FROM MONDRAGON TO AMERICA

Experiments in Community Economic Development

Greg MacLeod

University College of Cape Breton Press
Sydney, Nova Scotia
1997

Copyright Greg MacLeod, 1997

The University College of Cape Breton Press acknowledges the support received for its publishing program from the Canada Council's Block Grants program.

Cover design by Goose Lane Editions
Book design by Gail MacEachern
Printed and bound in Canada by City Printers, Sydney, N.S.

Canadian Cataloguing in Publication Data

MacLeod, Greg
 From Mondragon to America
 Includes bibliography references and index.
 ISBN 0-920336-53-1

Cooperative societies -- Spain -- Mondragon. 2. Community Development Corporations. I. Title.

   HD3218.M66M341997 334.6 C97 950197-0

University College of Cape Breton Press
Box 5300
Sydney, Nova Scotia
Canada B1P 6L2

*Dedicated to the memory of José Miguel Mancisidor
and The Reverend José Maria Mendizabal*

"Corporate values are the expression of the personality of the corporation, its commitment and a guide for the conduct of its members and a basis for commercial success. This value-based mode of behavior identifies the character of the corporation and distinguishes it from others. The collective living out of its values is what gives sense to the corporation. These values ought to be known and practiced by all members of the corporation, such that the individual and collective conduct will be in accord with the corporate mission."

José Ramon Fernandez

TU Lankide #398, Jan. 1996, p. 5.

CONTENTS

ACKNOWLEDGEMENTS

The information and ideas expressed in this book are culled from a variety of sources. The basic authority on the foundational ideas for Mondragon is a published university thesis by José Azurmendi: "El Hombre Cooperativo" (Cooperative Man). This study was published by the Mondragon Caja in 1984.

The other main sources are the archives at Ikasbide, assembled by the late Reverend José Maria Mendizabal, a copy of which is available at the University College of Cape Breton; the magazine *TU Lankide*, published by the Mondragon group; and the general works listed in the bibliography.

To gather firsthand information, I have visited Mondragon on at least eight occasions, and Valencia four times, while leading Canadian study-tours composed of leaders in community economic development.

I wish to thank Jesus Larranaga, one of the founders, and Juan Leibar, former president of the Escuela Polyteknika for their patient explanations. Also, I wish to acknowledge the kindness of José Maria Mendizabal, who spent a summer in Cape Breton. José Maria was the assistant to Arrizmendiarrieta and edited his writings. The staff of Ikasbide-Otalora was especially gracious to me. I cherish in a special way the memory of the late José Miguel Mancisidor who so impressed me with his Basque blend of incisive intellectual insight, loyalty and practicality.

I also wish to acknowledge the editorial assistance of Sister Stephanie Vincec, CSJ (Hamilton) in preparing this book for publication.

ABSTRACT

CHAPTER ONE describes the facts about Mondragon, what the visitor will see on a visit there or what one will read in the annual business report of the Caja Laboral Popular (Credit Union or Cooperative Bank) which for many years served as the glue to hold the complex together. The description includes how the components function and relate to one another. Mondragon exists as a concrete, functioning and profitable enterprise.

CHAPTER TWO explains how the strength and success of Mondragon is rooted in the founders' vision of society and their guiding value system. Aggressive expansion in response to community needs is seen as a virtue. The complex techniques of enterprise creation are described in detail. Also analyzed is their freedom from bankruptcy.

CHAPTER THREE responds to interest in the original intentions and innovative ideas that gave rise to all this activity. The researcher will find that none of the components is original but that each was proposed by some earlier thinker.[1] The genius of Don José Maria was to construct out of these elements an original synthesis which proved to be applicable to the world in which he lived. Syntheses are extremely important for the advancement of knowledge. The synthesis of ideas behind Mondragon is important because it triggered a collaboration among a variety of institutions that are normally divided and in competition.

CHAPTER FOUR contains a critique of different models for a business enterprise: capitalist, communist or communitarian. With the fall of the communist systems in Eastern Europe these questions are important. An extremely simplistic attitude might assume that the capitalist model has 'won.' However, problems like chronic unemployment, pollution, and events such as the Los Angeles riots, indicate that traditional capitalist systems have not provided a formula for human wellbeing.

CHAPTER FIVE presents the new model as envisaged by Don José Maria, the communitarian model which has yet to be widely tried in the Western world. An examination of its success in the Mondragon complex reveals that it is neither simply cooperative nor simply capitalist. The chapter shows how Mondragon takes elements from several models and results in a community-based business system which is very flexible and adaptable to changing social needs and circumstances.

CHAPTER SIX describes the Valencia experiment as an example of the transferability of Don José Maria's model. Founded by a group describing itself as followers of the Mondragon approach, the Valencian experiment consists of a community bank, a string of cooperative retail stores, an insurance company, employee-owned factories and a professional school.

CHAPTER SEVEN examines how the original motivation which inspired the Mondragon experiment is shared by many groups in North America, including one in Mexico, who are struggling to fight unemployment and economic decline in their own communities. Also discussed are examples of other community businesses which contain, in various degrees, some of the values associated with the Mondragon experiment.

CHAPTER EIGHT explains how technology is a way of thinking and a way of organizing. Based on his involvement in community economic development in Atlantic Canada during two decades, as well as his visits to the Spanish projects, the author proposes that basic guiding values and good technology are essential in making a new economy for a sustainable future.

Appendix II is a useful list of the 96 member-enterprises of the Mondragon Cooperative Corporation, including product lines and addresses.

Notes
1. This bears out the observation of the philosopher A.N. Whitehead, that all the philosophy written since the Classical Grecian era consists only of footnotes to Plato.

PROLOGUE

by Juan Leibar of Mondragon

In order to see the forest, you have to step back a distance; it is only in so doing that you can take in the woods and contemplate it as a whole.

The major work of Don José Maria Arrizmendiarrieta, which we call the "Cooperative Experiment" in Mondragon, has broken the boundaries of our small Basque Country, and has had remarkable repercussions abroad. An "experiment" which almost passed unnoticed at home has become the object of serious and rigorous studies by experts who have come from all corners of the world: Sweden, Japan, Argentina, the United States and Canada...to name only a few.

Of the many who have visited us, perhaps Greg MacLeod has been the one with the most persistence and dedication. His winsome presence has been very well received by all in the cooperative nerve centers: Caja Laboral, Eskola Politeknika, Otalora (the education centre for the Mondragon Cooperative Corporation), etc. His presence has become so familiar to us that we have affectionately named him "Don Gregorio," giving him a proper Spanish title.

As a result of his frequent visits, extended stays, his many interviews and his "on site" research, this present book has emerged. It is a concise and thorough document. From now on, especially in the English speaking world, those persons seeking information about the thinking of Don José Maria Arrizmendiarrieta regarding the "Experiment of Mondragon" and of its many accomplishments will have an excellent source of documentation.

Jesus Larranaga, one of the first disciples of Don José Maria, has written an interesting book with the theme: "In Search of a Way". He traces what Don José Maria did during all of his life: he searched for ways of developing more natural and universal principles. He fled from all dogmatism, unchangeable doctrines, ossified attitudes and old fashioned theories falsely promoted as religion. Many times he repeated, both directly and indirectly, that work is not to be thought of as a punishment but as an instrument with which to complete the work of the creator. Creation is incomplete, as much in its technologies as in its religious and social aspects. If Don José Maria had one fundamental, irrevocable principle, it was the message of Christ which he had taken on as a priest: "Love God above all things and your neighbour as yourself." That, and how to be human—nothing more. His was the classic principle: "to give to each one his or her due, to do harm to no one and to live honestly."

The "Experiment" was not designed in the abstract. It grew out of other experiments. As early as 1943, Don José Maria founded the Polytechnical School; at the same time he worked with the youth of Mondragon in social-economic activities such as the Young Christian Workers, the Workers Fraternity of Christian Action, Sports for Youth, etc.

Then, without following the dogmas of co-operativism, he used the cooperative formula to set up the first industrial enterprise, called ULGOR, in 1956. Instead, he followed some very simple principles such as:

a) the primacy of work over capital, without diminishing the importance of money, which is an indispensable element,

b) equality of all members - giving one vote to each member, while avoiding egalitarianism so that they could allow a differential in wages in a ratio of one to three;

c) supremacy of the General Assembly with solidarity in every thing so that paternalism is avoided;

d) money invested in education brings the highest of profits,

.... and so on.

In summary, he organized an "EXPERIMENT," which, like all experiments, has allowed for many different formulations; an experiment in the "here and now" which is not necessarily transferable as it exists here, neither to other places nor to other times.

We are reminded of a road. We have come so far and tomorrow we will continue, exploring the terrain and adapting to the circumstances which will arise.

I do not wish to close without congratulating "Don Gregorio," hoping that this "experiment" of Mondragon may inspire experiments in Canada.

Finally, I wish to remind him of lines written by the poet, Machado: "Walking, there is no road; The road is made by walking."

Juan Leibar, is a former professor and secretary-general of the Mondragon Polytechnical College which is a cooperative and member of the Mondragon Cooperative Corporation. Juan joined the College in 1957 and was closely associated with Don José Maria, the founder. Juan serves on the editorial board of the magazine TU Lankide, the official organ of the MCC.

INTRODUCTION

THE MONDRAGON IDEA HAS LEGS

Dr. Jimmy Tompkins of Cape Breton (where I live) frequently stated that it is not enough to have ideas, but that we have to put legs on our ideas. Among his own ideas to grow legs, Tompkins founded the first Credit Union in English-speaking Canada in 1933. Also, he organized the first cooperative housing group in Canada as well as the first regional library in Nova Scotia. Most importantly, Tompkins challenged institutions of learning to provide the intellectual and scientific leadership for economic reform.

This book is about a certain idea for economic reform and how it grew particular legs with the help of intellectual and scientific backing. The idea came from a Basque priest named Don José Maria, whose thinking bears a remarkable resemblance to that of Tompkins. Don José Maria often said that if ideas did not lead to action they were of no value. Don José Maria's remarkable achievement was to put legs on his ideas in the form of the Mondragon family of enterprises.

The Mondragon complex of companies in the Basque region of Spain, with over 30,000 workers and over six billion dollars in annual sales, has attracted international attention. By linking businesses, university and research institutes into one operational organism, with their own cooperative bank, Mondragon has created a synergy which has been extremely effective in generating new businesses and jobs. For example, Mondragon leaders projected the creation of 8,000 new jobs from 1996 to 2000.

Besides being an economic achievement, the Mondragon experiment is a fascinating social experiment. The total complex is owned by the workers and the customers. Further, an over-riding altruistic sense of community responsibility dominates the total system. In an age of disillusionment with the prevalent social economic systems, the achievements in Mondragon have had a tremendous attraction for reform-minded people in the Western world. Each of Mondragon's business enterprises, as well as any one of its related institutions, is worthy of study in itself, but most intriguing of all is the combination of all these elements into an organic whole. This is a case par excellence of the totality being greater than the sum of the parts. The Mondragon idea definitely has legs.

Why is this book necessary when a number of observers have already written about Mondragon? Because, in analyzing the Mondragon complex in terms of their own particular interests, these writers have neglected a crucial element, namely its basis in Judaeo-Christian values. For example, writers have discussed the experience in the light of the British labour movement, in the light of French cooperative history, in terms of the Marxist tradition, and in one enlightening work, comparing the strategies to those of Mahatma Ghandi.

To date, however, no one has focused on the Judaeo-Christian values underlying Mondragon. In this work I attempt to uncover that crucial missing element by describing this cooperative Mondragon experiment in terms of the ideas, intentions and methodology of its founder, Don José Maria. I do this in the context of my own observations concerning the history of the modern business corporation and my interest in applying basic Judaeo-Christian values to the concrete world in which we live, including the world of business. I believe that Don José Maria Arrizmendiarrieta, to whom I shall refer as Don José Maria, drew his ideas from the same Biblical source.

One basic point is that the intentions of Mondragon's founding group were altruistic and community-oriented. This flies in the face of the Hobbes-Smith tradition which holds that the 'rational' economic person acts out of pure self-interest. The defenders of the thesis that business is driven by pure egoism claim that experience proves them to be correct. This is to ignore the evidence of Mondragon, which is not simply an idea but living, empirical proof that alternative forms of business based on communitarian ideals can and do work. The founder, Don José Maria, agreed with the adage "It is not enough to understand the world, we must change it," and he put his new synthesis into a viable form which anyone can examine.

A second basic point is my belief that altruistic and community-oriented businesses can be set up elsewhere in the world. Many observers acknowledge the empirical results of Don José Maria's ideas but question the international relevance of the experiment. I disagree with the charge that the Mondragon experiment is nontransferable because of its commitment to a particular society.

I believe that commentators from a traditional economic point of view have missed the point. They have ignored the fact that the key to all of these community-based economic developments are the values rooted in a particular society, not neutral ideas and techniques claimed to be independent of social context.

If a value system constitutes the defining characteristic explaining the success of these ventures, then I argue that the essential elements are transferable. The key is not how to develop neutral ideas and techniques independent of social context but rather to root communitarian values into a particular society. To refute criticism of transferability, I have added two chapters about contemporary cases where groups seem to be using approaches that tend in the same direction as Mondragon.

The largest and most conscious attempt at transferability is the experiment in Valencia, Spain. A chapter describes how a team of social reformers adapted the Mondragon approach to a region with a different history and a different language. Valencia provides an empirical test of claims for transferability. Another chapter presents some interesting, though more tentative, examples from America.

Libraries abound with ideas and theory concerning economic reform. Admittedly, however, the many volumes simply do not have enough real life examples showing how reform minded people actually set up and operate businesses based upon a community oriented ethic. Thus the distance between the current economy and the wonderful ideals proposed by armchair theorists leads to paralysis.

This book contains the kind of concrete examples that are useful for activists seeking to learn a better way to do business. None of these examples are perfect. Yet they are doable. While choosing Mondragon as the most impressive, the number of other examples demonstrates the possibility of transferability.

From all of these the reader can pick and choose what constitutes best practice. Every community is unique and, in the end, each community will develop its own unique form of community based business. My hope in producing this volume is that these ideas will grow legs in other contexts.

CHAPTER 1

INSIDE MONDRAGON

A: BACKGROUND

First Impressions

As the world-wide economic crisis worsened in the 1990s an increasing number of politicians, labour leaders and academics began a desperate search for new solutions. Now willing to look at alternative approaches to business, many visited Mondragon, an economic model which has functioned in the Basque region of Spain since 1956. Expecting a community based business to be amateur and small scale, they were usually surprised. One North American professor, David Schweickart,[1] who made a visit in 1994, wrote in a letter:

Suddenly, we enter a valley, and there's this town—I'd guess of about 50,000. It's a pretty, prosperous looking town. Lots of new housing being built, a couple of nicely kept parks. But clearly a working-class town: no tourist shops, no signs for pensions, nothing ostentatious or luxurious. And there on the side of the mountain, overlooking the town are a couple of buildings I recognize from the video I'd seen.[2]

So we drive up. No gates or security guards. Here we are at the headquarters of MCC, the **Mondragon Corporacion Cooperativa** *(its new name, since 1986). Close by is the central office of the Caja Laboral Popular [bank], and a separate building that houses the bank's data processing center. A little further down the mountain is Ikerlan, their research center. Further down still is Lagun-Aro, their private social-security facility and at the base, the Eskola Politeknika.*

One is struck by how non-flashy it all is. All the buildings are of a modern (not post-modern) functional design. The grounds are well-kept, but everything looks just a bit run down. And wide open. We don't try to go into the buildings, but we wander all around them, taking pictures, etc. There are a couple of cars parked nearby, and we meet an old couple out for a stroll, but no cops or watchmen or anything. And yet, as we learn later:

- *MCC is a more important economic player in the Basque region (the whole region, not just this little town) than GM is in the U.S.;*
- *Ikerlan is the only Spanish research firm to have met the NASA technical specifications and hence permitted a project on the Columbia space shuttle last summer;*
- *Caja Laboral Popular has been rated as among the 100 most efficient financial institutions in the world in terms of its profit/asset ratio;*
- *the Eskola Politeknika, enrolling 2,000 students, is considered the best technical institute in Spain;*
- *MCC's distribution branch, Eroski, opened more "hypermarkets" than any other retailing group in the country;*
- *MCC's capital goods division is the market leader in metal cutting tools in Spain, as is its division that makes refrigerators, washing machines and dishwashers;*
- *MCC engineers have built "turnkey"[3] factories in China, North Africa, the Middle East and in Latin America.*

All in all MCC has a workforce of over 30,000, and financial assets of about $8 billion. Frankly, it's hard to believe, standing on the steps of the modest little building that is the general headquarters, that all this could be true. But apparently it is.

It's also true that these are extraordinarily hard times in the Basque region, which is in the middle of the deepest economic recession it has experienced since World War II. Official unemployment is about 25%. Indeed, employment in the MCC industrial cooperatives has fallen from 17,000 in 1991 to 15,000 now—though overall employment in MCC has not fallen. It's still quite rare, our San Sebastian colleagues tell us, for a person to actually lose his or her job. Cutbacks are effected through reassignment to other cooperatives and through non-replacement of retirees.

The big culprit here, of course, is the usual suspect: global capitalism—in this case Spain's incorporation into the European Economic Union, which has greatly intensified competition. Which brings me to the downside of MCC. While the good news is that it is surviving (it's showing itself able to compete in the Brave New World of hypermobile capital) its sense of itself as a radically different form of economic organization, as a pioneer opening up new possibilities—that's not what it once was. "Let's face it," said Balaren (the economist from San Sebastian), "MCC is now just another multinational corporation." I'm not sure that's quite right. The woman who showed us around Ikerlan expressed a similar sentiment, but when asked if it was important to be a member of the cooperative rather than a contract laborer, her reply was immediate, "Oh yes. As members we have job security. And we get to vote."

I'm not as dismayed by the resemblance between MCC and a multinational firm as many are, because I've never viewed Mondragon as the seed from which, by a process of spontaneous multiplication, a new economic order would be born.[4] Mondragon is important because it shows what is possible without capitalists. Democratically structured enterprises can be technically sophisticated and highly efficient. Mondragon continues to prove that point. But capitalism will never be brought down by some process of peaceful, fair competition with worker-owned firms. Because the competition will never be fair. Not when capitalism can scour the world for low wages and compliant governments.

So I actually feel good about Mondragon. Under extremely difficult circumstances, it's surviving. Economically it is not in crisis. That's good. I'm pleased. I only wish I'd had more time there to talk to more people.

Like Professor Schweickart we can all feel good about Mondragon. Its achievement provides an empirical, real world example of capital and, more importantly, of technology being used other than for the enrichment of non-resident shareholders. The Mondragon case is a great confirmation for those who believe that the only rational goal for business and technology is worker as well as community improvement.

Thumbnail History

To understand what the Mondragon business complex is all about, we must go back to 1956 when five young engineers in this Basque country of northern Spain, inspired by the ideas of Don José Maria, set up a small enterprise to produce oil stoves. With the help of their former teacher and pastor, they borrowed some money and went into production following principles of democratic decision making, profit sharing and community responsibility. They named the enterprise ULGOR, the first letter of each of their names.[5] This enterprise became successful in a very short time. When they needed further capital for expansion they formed a bank following the same principles of cooperative ownership. As each enterprise became successful and grew, it divided and sub-divided to create a complex of inter-related worker-owned enterprises that is still growing.

From 1975 to 1985 the whole Basque region, like most of the western world, suffered through a severe economic crisis. During this period the region lost 150,000 jobs. In contrast the Mondragon complex gained over four thousand jobs. Moreover, by 1986, the Mondragon complex was clearly a player on the international scene. At this time the leaders decided to re-define themselves to reflect more accurately their new reality. Instead of simply calling themselves a cooperative they began to call themselves the **Mondragon Cooperative Corporation, (MCC).**

To most economists, the name is a contradiction in terms. How can a business "corporation" be, at the same time, an apparently opposite entity, a "cooperative"? This apparent oxymoron is reason enough to explain why so many people wish to know more details of this remarkable experiment.

Most readers are familiar with consumer cooperatives such as grocery stores and credit unions. The cooperative business tradition, rooted in nineteenth-century Europe, is based on the notion of ordinary citizens controlling the businesses upon which they depend, thus making a better life for all. In this system each shareholder has only one vote regardless of the amount of money invested. In Europe and America most cooperatives are owned by the customers. Ownership by employees in the form of worker cooperatives is a relatively new development. Thus, when the organizers of the ULGOR Company proposed that all the workers should be the owners with one vote each in a cooperative structure, they were breaking new ground in the general cooperative tradition.

Although the founders of ULGOR were attracted to the democratic principles of the cooperative business tradition, they were realistic. They recognized the weakness of traditional cooperatives in their tendency to be isolationist and marginal in the main economy. To prevent debilitating fragmentation in their new enterprises, they insisted that each of the new businesses they set up should remain linked together as associated cooperative businesses. To this day, unity is maintained through interlinked boards and joint agreements.

As will become obvious by the end of this chapter, there has been a tremendous increase in size and complexity since 1956. In an organic fashion new branches have developed and then branches of the branches, yet the interlinkages have been maintained.

In order to appreciate the measure of this achievement it is important to walk through the system step by step while remembering that the complex began with practically no initial investment. This is important in the context of Spain where individuals who started most new businesses had access to capital accumulated over several generations. By contrast, the founders of ULGOR were working class people without great inherited wealth. Their only possibility of raising capital was to go to the people. The unusual result is that we now have a world class, high tech cooperative corporation depending upon the *local community* for capitalization. It is an international monument to the power of community moral support when it is expressed in the form of financial backing. Unlike much of the North American experience, where social reformers have been slow to appreciate the value and even the essential role of capital and technology, the ULGOR founders used both in the creation of a new social order. This unique combination is still evident in the Mission Statement and Operating Guidelines (to be discussed in Chapter 2).

B: MONDRAGON: THE PARTS

The 1996 Annual Report describes the key elements (parts) of the corporation. These are divided into four enterprise groups: Financial, Industrial, Distribution and Corporate, with the entire system unified under one umbrella organization called the Congress.

I. Financial Group (6 enterprises)

At a time when most large corporations were in economic recession, the asset base of the Mondragon complex was growing. In 1996, assests were well over $13 billion and sales exceeded $6 billion a year.

The Financial Group includes the Caja Laboral Popular (equivalent to a credit union) and the Lagun Aro, a social security company, both of which are described below. The remaining enterprises are a variety of parafinancial companies involved in such activities as insurance and leasing.

The *Caja Laboral Popular* or Community Bank (credit union) is the core of Mondragon's financial enterprises.

Leaders in the Mondragon system freely admit that if they did not have their own banking system, their worker cooperatives could not exist today. In Europe many cooperatives failed over the years because traditional private banks were not prepared to support them in difficult times.

Mondragon executives cannot imagine a serious producer cooperative system without an associated bank. Throughout the years of the economic crisis the Mondragon system survived while many traditional companies went bankrupt.

From the first, the role of the Caja was clear: to utilize local financial resources and invest them in the creation of new enterprises for the development of the Basque region, which was suffering from high unemployment. The Caja's role was fundamentally a social mission. Although the Caja began with the double function of finance and new enterprise creation, eventually the role of business development was hived off to other parts.

With 125 branches under one board and one general manager this Caja has become very effective in attracting savings from the local area. With the motto "Savings or Suitcases" the Caja suggests that while money in a National Bank helps create jobs in Madrid, money in their bank (the Caja) helps to create jobs in the Basque country.[6]

The owner-members of the Caja are the employees and the associated cooperative enterprises. Each client-cooperative signs a Contract of Association which imposes strict obligations.

Contract of Association
1. The member enterprise must agree with the general principles of a cooperative as outlined by the Congress.
2. It must agree with the system of wage levels and ratios.
3. It must agree to a fixed interest on capital contributions.
4. It must invest in the Caja.
5. It must deposit all surplus cash and liquid assets with the Caja.
6. Surpluses or losses of the enterprise will be distributed according to a basic formula agreed on by the Congress. (The formula directs at least 20 percent of surplus to be retained by the enterprise for reserves, at least 10 percent to a social fund and the remainder to be distributed to worker members. The worker-share is deposited with the Caja and can only be taken out on retirement.)
7. It must agree to provide a five year budget and monthly statements to the Caja.
8. It must agree to an audit by the Caja at least every four years.

In effect, the associated co-ops are not permitted to deal with outside financial institutions. All pension funds, workers' share capital, social security funds and other benefits reside in the Caja and thus add significantly to the pool of savings placed there by individuals. Because of this strong equity base, the Caja was able to play a key role not only in developing new enterprises but also in devising imaginative rescue packages when an enterprise was in trouble. For example, it was not unusual for the Caja to propose an interest write-down on condition that the employee-members agreed to a contribution and a restructuring.

At the General Assembly of the Caja, 42 per cent of the votes are by the Caja employees and 58 per cent of the votes are by the enterprise clients. The Board of the Caja is structured with seven seats for the cooperative enterprises, four for the Caja employees and one for the Congress Board.

Lagun Aro (Social Security Facility) was established to meet the needs of employees in the Mondragon cooperative complex who are classed as self-employed and do not fall under the State. As well as providing unemployment benefits (downtime between job transfers), it provides medical service through a number of clinics. In 1982 an Insurance Division was added. The total social security system is based upon worker contributions with employees being able to choose among a variety of benefits which vary in levels of service and price.

II. Industrial Group (67 enterprises)

Whether the whole Mondragon complex started with the stove-making factory in 1956 or the trade school in 1943 is open to debate. There is no debate, however, that the main core of the system is made up of industrial producers. Numbering sixty-seven, these enterprises produce a vast range of products as diverse as automotive parts, domestic appliances such as refrigerators, stoves and dishwashers, bicycles and bus bodies. Further, they also do a great deal of construction. One of their companies built the Sant Jordi Sports Arena in Barcelona for the 1992 Olympics. They have also built factories in Brazil and China on a turnkey basis.

Although from the point of view of capital, the main construction has been commercial, domestic housing has not been neglected. In 1986 there were seventeen housing cooperatives containing 1,100 living units, associated with the Credit Union. Although the apartment buildings are built cooperatively, individuals own their own apartments and may sell them. The group has also established a cooperative enterprise to produce prefabricated homes.

Besides the 67 enterprises owned by the employees in the Basque region, the MCC has developed and acquired 13 subsidiary enterprises during the 1990s. As indicated in the appendix the percentage of ownership varies. For instance "Extra Electromenager" is a capitalistic company engaged in producing refrigerators in Morocco. Fifty-one percent of the shares are owned by FAGOR, a worker-owned cooperative in Mondragon. This is an example of the MCC adaptation to the pressures of the new international economy.

III. Distribution (8 enterprises)

Two of the main enterprises that distribute goods for Mondragon are Eroski and Lankide Export.

Eroski, which has 264 stores, dominates the Consumer Sector. The bulk of sales by this large consumer cooperative is in groceries and furniture. Ninety-eight of the stores are owned by the co-op and the remainder are privately owned, operating under a franchise and being supplied by the Eroski warehouse. The Eroski chain is the largest distributor of food in the Basque provinces and the third largest in Spain. Recently, Eroski made an agreement with the "Consum" cooperative retail system of Valencia so that they are now one giant system. (The Valencia experiment will be discussed in Chapter 6.) The Eroski sign now marks a familiar institution around Northern Spain where both members and non-members shop. Of course, Eroski sells more than groceries. Furniture produced in the cooperative factories is available through this system.

The original idea of the retail system was to sell goods produced by the Mondragon cooperative complex. This is in strong contrast to most North American cooperative retail stores which see their role as simply delivering cheaper groceries and thereby helping the consumer. The genius of the Mondragon system is that it is not necessary to opt for either the consumer or the producer but to link them both in one complex organization. The founders have thereby shown that it is possible to devise a system that respects the rights of both producer and consumer, both sides of the economic equation.

To assure efficiency and to promote cross community unity, Eroski has one board of directors composed of twelve persons and one general manager for all the branches. However, each store has local committees who concentrate on consumer education and product improvement. The General Assembly, which elects the board, is balanced between employees and consumer-members, with each having 50 per cent of the votes. The Eroski board is composed of six employees and six consumers, but the chairperson must be a consumer.

Lankide Export was set up in 1980 as an agency to support the export process. The importance of exporting was accentuated with Spain's entry into the Common Market. In 1995 over 15 per cent of the total Mondragon sales was through export.[7] Through its own sales offices and other commercial companies, it promotes and sells products, arranges trade and barter contracts and participates in international trade fairs. Besides the sale of industrial products, this agency arranges turnkey factory construction contracts in other countries such as China, and co-invests in mixed manufacturing companies.

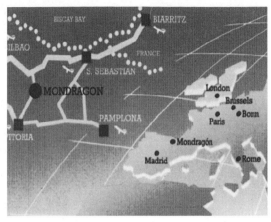

IV. Corporate Activities (15 enterprises)

Under the heading of corporate activities are fifteen enterprises which have been established to serve the total commercial complex as well as the community in general. These are second level cooperatives in that they include other cooperative enterprises as voting members. Their role is to promote, assist and develop new and existing enterprises. As second-level organizations, their boards are hybrid, involving employees and clients. This avoids the possibility of the producer exploiting the consumer or the consumer exploiting the producer. The most important activities of this group are in the area of education and research.

The League of Education and Culture

The League of Education and Culture (now called *Hezibide Elkartea*) is a grouping of thirteen different educational centres, with 6,303 students at different levels. Three of these centres are at university level. The largest centre is the polytechnical university which specializes in Production Engineering, Computer Technology, Microelectronics and Industrial Electronics. Attached to it is the new Centre for Industrial Design.

Higher Education

Education, in all its senses, general, technical and adult, has been a creative force in the whole complex from the first. *Alecoop*, a student enterprise, is a cooperative industry which started as a spinoff from the Polytechnical University. Students work half the day in the factory and study in the university during the other half of the day.

Ikasbide or Otalora is a residential learning centre for management that provides postgraduate management training. When it became clear that university graduates were not appropriately prepared for the Mondragon type of enterprise, a two year program was developed with on-the-job training as a central component. In 1990 eighty-one candidates were selected from 1,500 applications. Ikasbide has a wide variety of in-service programs for managers, such as marketing, communications and finance, and an educational program for Boards of Directors of the various cooperative enterprises in the Mondragon system.

Besides the above regular programs, Otalora houses the monthly magazine about Mondragon called *TU Lankide*. Also, this centre serves as a contact with many universities and groups in other countries.

Elementary Schools

Not to be overlooked is the Mondragon role in primary education. When the business enterprises were set up in the 1950s, Dictator Franco refused to allow education in the Basque language. Mondragon leaders saw the preservation of their traditional language as a fundamental part of their development mission. Thus they devoted a percentage of their earnings to the establishment of schools in the villages where the Basque language could be taught. By 1985, there were thirty-five Basque-speaking schools with thirty-five thousand students, organized and supported by the Mondragon cooperative system. In the period after the democratization of Spain, many of these schools were eventually taken over by the local government authorities who were now pro-Basque. Some remain in the Mondragon system.

The involvement of the Mondragon industrial complex in education indicates an important element in the philosophy of total development, namely, that the final purpose is always the integral development of the local people. If the local culture were seen to be threatened, then most likely the cooperative corporate leaders would again devote funds and take initiatives to protect the local community.

Research Institutes

A variety of research institutes such as *Ikerlan* are located under the Mondragon corporate umbrella and they are governed as a cooperative. They began as services developed by the Polytechnical University. Since their main purpose has always been the development of enterprises, they will be treated in Chapter 2 under "Enterprise Creation."

MCC Overview			
Year	1994	1995	1996
Total Assets	$ 10.8 billion	$ 12.3 billion	$ 13.8 billion
Total Sales	$ 4.9 billion	$ 5.5 billion	$ 6.0 billion
Exports	$ .8 billion	$ 1.0 billion	$ 1.1 billion
Personnel	25,990	27,950	29,407
Source: Mondragon Annual Reports			

C. STRUCTURES AND GOVERNANCE

The preceding section described some of the elements within the Mondragon complex. By now the reader should have a clear picture of the breadth and complexity of this unique cooperative corporation. Most readers are familiar with the traditional cooperative system where all members have one vote each in electing a board of directors to represent their interests. The board in turn hires a manager who is responsible for the day to day activities of the enterprise.

From here on in, the Mondragon structure becomes much more complex. It resembles a set of Russian dolls.

At the **basic level** are individuals who belong to an individual cooperative. Then a group of cooperatives belong to a zone grouping or division, which is the **second level**. All of the enterprises and organizations, such as the University, belong to the Congress, which is the **third level**. The Congress is the supreme authority.

In contrast to traditional cooperatives which tend to guard their autonomy and operate independently of their neighbouring cooperative enterprises, the Mondragon cooperatives are intricately interlaced together to form mutually supporting systems at many levels. A manager of an Eroski consumer store may be on the board of directors of the Congress. The chairperson of an educational cooperative enterprise may be a salesperson in another cooperative enterprise.

As well as political interdependency among the cooperatives, there is financial interdependency. Individual cooperative enterprises contribute to common funds that provide support when one enterprise is in difficulty. Also, all of the cooperative enterprises in one zone may share in one educational or cultural project. Technically, each cooperative enterprise is independent and can vote to leave the system. However, this possibility is largely theoretical because, in reality, so many contractual obligations and financial dependencies exist that severance becomes unthinkable. The structure is such that the whole complex functions as one giant corporation with many interdependent parts and divisions.

Operational Structures of Governance

The total Mondragon structure, which depends upon the individual persons who constitute the membership, rests upon a very simple but fundamental principle: alone, each person is weak, but individuals united as a group become strong. The main operational structures of governance described below are three: the single enterprise, the Zone or Division Group and the General Congress.

Operational Structures 1. SINGLE ENTERPRISE

General Assembly. Every worker-member of a Mondragon enterprise is a shareholder and has the right to vote at the annual General Assembly of the enterprise held once a year. The two main functions of the General Assembly are to approve the operational plan for the year and to elect replacements to a board of nine directors.

Board of Directors. The by-laws require more than one candidate for each board seat so there is never an election of a board member by acclamation. A board member sits for four years with half the members replaced every two years. The assembly also elects a supervisory-audit committee. Each of the 96 worker-owned enterprises functions in the same way.

The board presents the operational plan to the Assembly for approval. The General Assembly elects two bodies to which it delegates specified authority. The main body elected is the board of directors. The board hires the manager, holds monthly meetings and is responsible for monitoring the day to day operation. The other body elected by the Assembly is the supervisory committee which audits the books and reports directly to the assembly concerning the finances. It is an open-book system so that the workers know where the money goes.

Two further bodies are appointed by each enterprise but these are internal operational committees, the Management Council and the Social Council.

The Management Council consists of the heads of key departments such as Finance, Production, Personnel and Marketing, and serves as an advisory body, as well as a communications channel to the manager, who is appointed by the Board.

Manager. The board is required to have at least three candidates for the position of manager. This is a technique designed to prevent the entrenchment of one management clique. The appointment is for four years.

Once the manager is appointed he or she is responsible for all operating decisions. The board and committees advise, but the manager has to

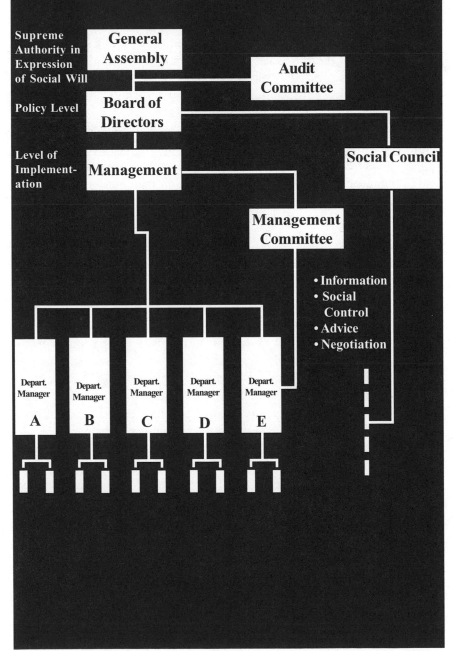

BASIC STRUCTURE OF A WORKERS' COOPERATIVE

Supreme Authority in Expression of Social Will

General Assembly

Audit Committee

Policy Level

Board of Directors

Level of Implementation

Management

Social Council

Management Committee

- Information
- Social Control
- Advice
- Negotiation

Depart. Manager A

Depart. Manager B

Depart. Manager C

Depart. Manager D

Depart. Manager E

bear responsibility for decisions. If worker-members are dissatisfied with the manager, then they can convoke a General Assembly with 20 per cent of the workers signing a petition. The General Assembly can dismiss the manager or require a new operational plan.

The Social Council performs the functions normally performed by a labour union. Each department, for example, electrical or marketing, elects a delegate to the Social Council somewhat in the sense of a shop-steward. The Social Council has no management authority. The total money available for wages is decided by the board; this is generally called the "envelope system" in large institutions. It is up to the Social Council to decide how the wage envelope is to be divided.

Besides advising both the board and the manager concerning general working conditions, the Social Council makes decisions concerning a broad range of personnel issues such as health, benefits and safety. It is an important communications instrument, channelling information from management to workers and from workers to management.

Economic Aspects

Three economic aspects of a Mondragon enterprise differentiate it radically from arrangements in a traditional corporation; they concern the system of wages, internal economics and profit-sharing.

Wages. The early founders invented a system of dividing wages in a way that was fair and equitable according to a numerical ratio. No one person was allowed to earn more than three times what another person earned. In 1986 the ratio was increased to become six to one. When the ratio was raised to 6:1 from 3:1 there was a great deal of debate at the annual meeting of the Congress. There was a reluctance to create greater social divisions. However, it was decided that higher wages were necessary in order to attract more highly skilled specialists.

Effectively most groups follow a ratio of 4:1 and the few people in the higher range are exceptional. We shall use the four to one as a model. It is the responsibility of the elected Social Council to assign numerical values to the roles of each worker. For instance, a new, unskilled worker may be given the classification of 1.00. If the worker gains a technical diploma then .1 may be added, and if the worker becomes responsible for a work team then another .3 may be added, so that his co-efficient is now 1.4. Points are also added for years worked. The manager may be classed as 4 and earn $60,000 while the file-clerk, classed as 1, earns $15,000. An engineer may be classified as 3 and thus her wage would automatically be $45,000. To determine the classification between 1 and 4, a wide variety of factors are considered, such as education, seniority, supervisory responsibility and performance evaluation.

Internal Economics. To become a worker-member, a person must make two contributions of an economic nature:

1) personal ability which is tested during a probationary period

2) a capital contribution which is normally one year's wages for an unskilled worker (from $10-15 thousand). The worker may borrow the money from the Caja or arrange a check-off.

The salary of each worker-member is never fixed absolutely. At the beginning of each year, a figure is set which seems reasonable in the light of anticipated earnings of the enterprise.

Profit-Sharing. Any profits which remain after salaries and other expenses are then divided up in a pre-determined fashion.

A typical division of profits might be:

    10% to the Social-Cultural Fund
    20% to the company reserve fund
    70% to the worker-members

The use of the Social-Cultural Fund is flexible and ranges from support of community schools to staff development. The company reserve-fund becomes a permanent part of the company equity and can never be withdrawn by the employees. The other 70 per cent of the profits go to the personal capital account of each member-worker. During years of loss it is possible that the worker's capital account will be reduced. The individual worker only receives this money upon retirement or when leaving the company. An average worker, after twenty-five years service would receive a lump sum of approximately $100,000 plus a pension which would be equivalent to approximately 70 per cent of average earnings during the last five years. Pensions are set and do not depend upon profit and loss.

Operational Structures: 2. THE DIVISIONS or ZONES

A number of individual industrial enterprises producing related products are normally grouped together to form a division or zone group. Thus, those enterprises making refrigerators, washers, stoves and such have been organized into the Home Appliance Division even though each is a legally independent worker-owned enterprise. In another zone, most of the member enterprises may be producing agricultural and food products.

The General Assembly of the divison consists of delegates appointed by the General Assembly of each individual enterprise in the zone. Unlike the General Assembly of a single enterprise, however, the role of the Zone

General Assembly is not to elect a board. The Zone Assembly approves the general operational guidelines for the zone group.

A General Board of the zone group is constituted by each individual enterprise naming their own board chairperson and one board member-at-large. The managers of all the individual enterprises form a management committee and the General Board of the zone usually picks one of them to serve as a general manager for the group. The linkages then are horizontal rather than hierarchical.

Although each enterprise is legally independent, the Divisional General Board, in the name of its individual enterprises, exercises authority in certain areas, such as common wage guidelines for the zone. If an individual enterprise does not abide by such guidelines then that enterprise would be excluded from the group. The authority of the zone board and the zone manager is over matters that affect all member enterprises. These would include such matters as a common brand name, advertising, group purchasing of material, group marketing and a common investment fund.

This division structure plays a key role in such areas as wage parities and a common reserve fund. During a recession, workers may be moved from one enterprise to another depending upon the need. In a spirit of mutual support, profits as well as losses are averaged out amongst the group. Thus it may be that one enterprise has a bad year, but the other enterprises will make up for these losses so that the individual worker will not suffer. Of course, all member enterprises must submit to the advice of a specialist corporate agency set up to analyze and ascertain necessary reforms when any one enterprise is in difficulty.

The economic role of this kind of structure is quite obvious. The group is a much stronger actor in the commercial world than each individual enterprise could be on its own.

Over the years, this second-order level of organization has evolved, often in response to trends in the international market place. In 1997, for instance, eight different cooperative enterprises, led by Fagor Ederlan, were selling components to multinationals such as General Motors, Ford, Volkswagon, Peugeot, Citroen, etc. These eight enterprises have constituted a sectoral group or division. Thus the zone system has evolved into a system of 7 divisions: Automotive, Home Appliances, Construction, Industrial Equipment, Domestic, Engineering and Machine Tools.

Operational Structures: 3.THE GENERAL CONGRESS

The third level of organization in the Mondragon complex is that of the General Congress. The General Congress (the general assembly of all

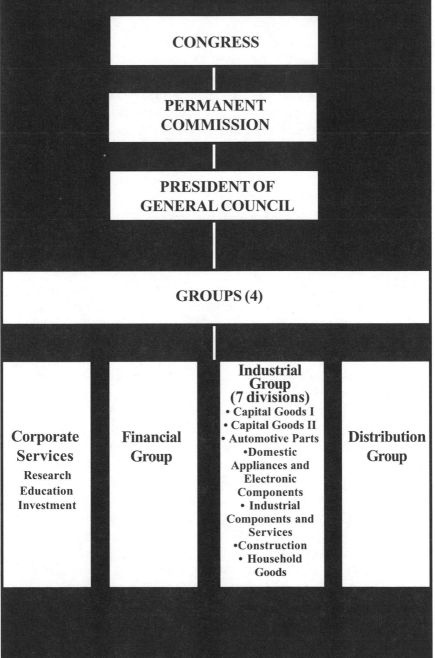

ORGANIZATIONAL STRUCTURE

CONGRESS

PERMANENT COMMISSION

PRESIDENT OF GENERAL COUNCIL

GROUPS (4)

Corporate Services

Research
Education
Investment

Financial Group

Industrial Group (7 divisions)
• Capital Goods I
• Capital Goods II
• Automotive Parts
•Domestic Appliances and Electronic Components
• Industrial Components and Services
•Construction
• Household Goods

Distribution Group

the cooperative enterprises and organizations) is the most powerful body in the system. It is made up of 350 delegates representing all of the members. The Congress meets once a year and approves the general operating plans and strategies presented by the Congress Board and thus gives policy direction.

The Congress Board is not elected directly. Rather, its 22 members are the general managers of the divisions plus delegates from special institutions such as the Caja, the Polytechnic College Erpski and the Research Institutions. The role of the Congress Board is administrative.

The General Congress evolved as a pragmatic response to new international developments. Until 1986 the Caja was the cement which held all the enterprise members together in a common structure. In 1986 however, the Congress structure was instituted as the result of the self-examination triggered by the need to prepare for the economic realities of the Common Market and the world scene of the 1990s. In Spain the Mondragon group holds 33 per cent of the market for refrigerators and stoves, but in the new Europe they hold only two per cent of the market. Leaders in the planning process perceived the need to develop a structure with a great deal of legitimacy that could develop new kinds of strategies to guide the total corporate complex. This is especially serious since the major corporations of Europe are continually dividing and regrouping in new corporate alliances. Even though all the companies and institutions in the Mondragon complex were inter-related and inter-linked, it was considered necessary to develop a structure that would permit rapid decision-making in strategic matters and, at the same time, be able to attain a consensus among the various components of the system.

An example of a key strategic decision for the Mondragon complex would be whether and how they can form alliances with traditional stock-owned companies such as Fabrelec Ltd., a privately owned Spanish company specializing in domestic appliances. This company has been judged to be useful in accessing Mexican and American markets. Since Mondragon is a community-owned corporate structure where each worker has one non-transferable share, to devise a system of international holding companies would require innovative structures and very good communications with the local worker-owners.

The shift from the Caja to the Congress, as a key unifying structure, has resulted in a natural shift of authority. The Congress now sets down the operational guidelines and the overall strategy. Members must abide by decisions made through the Congress, or else leave the system. Since leaving the system would deprive the enterprise of the total infrastructure support, this is not a viable option, even though it is a legal option. A typical rule binding all the enterprises is that no enterprise is allowed to go beyond the salary ratio scale of six-to-one. If an enterprise went to ten-to-one, then that enterprise would have to leave. However, they could decide upon a lesser ratio, such as three-to-one, and not break the rule. However, in recent years, the Congress has allowed some rare exceptions, permitting a higher salary in order to attract a highly specialized individual.

A very important function of the Congress is to orient the total Mondragon complex to meet the changing needs of the economic world. An example of this is the decision to devote $600 per worker per year to formation. This means that the member enterprises have to contribute approximately $15 million per year to formation. The Congress is very important in the task of developing consensus among the work-force and keeping all members informed about changing European conditions.

The Congress has assumed the responsibility of creating new enterprises and new jobs. To make that possible, every enterprise is obliged to contribute to a central investment pool. Currently, most of this pool is used in the reorganization and retooling of existing enterprises. The Caja provides investment capital for new enterprises. Since competitive European companies are merging to form new alliances, the Congress takes the responsibility for determining methods of collaborating with other non-Spanish companies to establish the equivalent of mergers.

When Spain entered the European Common Market, critics said the Mondragon system would not survive in such tough open competition. On the contrary, Mondragon has prospered and expanded, more than doubling its exports between 1991 and 1996.

On the other hand, the Mondragon leadership is sometimes criticized by social activists for doing business with foreign, capitalistic companies. The Mondragon response is that, given the need to perform in the international arena, they need to do business with the kinds of corporations that are there. Mondragon's leaders say that they would prefer to deal with community owned corporations but very few actually exist. They do collaborate with progressive groups in other countries such as Brazil who are attempting to develop the local economy. They simply deal with the capitalist companies in a purely commercial manner without attempting to act as missionaries promoting their own system.

Notes

1. Professor David Schweickart is a political science author and adjunct professer of political science at the University of Waterloo, in Ontario. He wrote this letter to a friend in 1994. Emphasis added.

2. A number of videos are available and may be ordered through the Department of Public Relations in Mondragon. Another video, "Mondragon: Community Business Series," by Greg MacLeod, producer, is available through BCA. Both addresses are in Appendix II.

3. Specifications will vary, but most "turnkey" arrangements involve complete construction and setting up of a manufacturing operation. When the factory is complete and the equipment is installed, the builder-contractor walks away and the owner-operator takes over.

4. As will become apparent in succeeding chapters, Mondragon is profoundly different. The basic purpose is local community improvement and not the enrichment of non-resident shareholders. While the resemblance to conventional multinationals is real at a superficial level, the huge difference becomes obvious when the board is faced with the necessity of closing down a redundant factory.

5. Their names are: Luis Usatorre, Jesus Larranaga, Alfonso Gorronogoitia, José Maria Ormaechea, Javier Ortubay.

6. Thus obviating the need of suitcases for their young to leave. During the past twenty years, governments in the Western World have spent billions of dollars as subsidies to attract industries to areas of high unemployment. Different government departments and programs have been set up and millions have been spent on studies. So far, the record in most countries is poor.

7. *Cf.* 1955, Annual Report, p. 9.

CHAPTER 2

THE STRENGTH OF MONDRAGON

Observers of Mondragon usually search for the secret formula. Thinking in terms of a mechanistic technique or some financial support system, they usually analyze at the wrong level. The answer is found in a category which should be classed as value systems. It concerns how we understand ourselves and our society. It is about choosing one way of life over another, choices that have been described in Don José Maria's thinking and in the "isms" that flourish in our world.

In a technology-driven world it is normal for people to expect all innovation and success to be a direct result of some new electronic or scientific discovery. The essence of technology is repetition. As the Greeks pointed out, when humans discover some secret of nature in terms of a way of doing things, and repeat that formula over and over again they are using technology. For the manufacture and operation of airplanes, manuals are provided and managers need only follow the instructions to achieve success. This is what technology is about. Thus, in most industrialized societies, technology drives economic development. Some new invention is discovered, and there is great pressure to implement it.

A: MISSION STATEMENT

But as valuable as it is, technology concerns "how to do things" and not "why we do things." In the case of Mondragon, where emphasis on technology is high, nevertheless the technology is driven by principles and values. The Mission Statement and the Operating Guidelines which flow from it are presented in the Annual Report of 1993. These are a clear illustration of the communitarian values upon which the whole complex is built.

Mission Statement

The Mondragon Cooperative Corporation is the embodiment of a social-economic experiment in the business world, the mission of which is the production and sale of goods, services and distribution. Democratic methods are used to elect the governing and management bodies on which the Corporation's organizational structure is based; and the material and social assets generated are distributed for the benefit of its members and the community, as a measure of solidarity.

To achieve the aims expressed in its mission, the MCC shall operate competitively, generating the resources necessary for harmonious development.

Operating Guidelines

1. CLIENT SATISFACTION

In the certitude that the user of our products and services is the ultimate rationale of our very existence as a business, let us respond to the needs of the client, foresee future needs and, with personalized attention, increase the level of client satisfaction.

2. PERSON CENTERED

So that the well known expression that people are the first and principal asset of the corporation may not be simply an empty, rhetorical phrase, but a lived reality. So that we encourage creativity, initiative and communication above property, obedience and pedigree, and where systematic programs of formation guarantee the permanent development of all the workers.

3. PRODUCTS AND SERVICES

We are conscious that the most objective form of appreciation and validation of our enterprise is through our products. Products, and the commercialization and servicing of them, makes possible the generation of resources sufficient for the consolidation and development of our corporation. The search for a full guarantee and the optimization of our services are factors that can help us to consolidate our postion in the the marketplace.

4. COOPERATION

In our cooperative model of shared management, the word "cooperation" takes on a broader meaning. It includes individual collaboration, collaboration of teams, and above all, participation in the corporation as a whole, dedicated to society but also efficient and competent. We share responsibilities, delegate functions and assume risks. We are involved in the processes of organization and as well, we share the satisfaction of fulfilling the objectives. These are the keys of cooperation together with respect for the pre-established rules of the game.

5. CONTINUAL IMPROVEMENT

With the continual search for optimization of systems and processes in a changing environment, the adaptation to new markets and the fulfillment of our committment to supply must be constant. The open character of our management, receptive to the necessities of new technologies, should serve as a catalyst to motivate the workers in each of our cooperatives to the task of continual improvement.

6. COMMUNITY COMMITMENT

So that we not become limited to the narrow confines of our individual cooperatives, but rather that we transcend our own group. To create jobs and create community wealth are the irrevocable requirements of our community vocation. And within this community commitment we must not forget to proclaim our respect for the ecosystem and the search for solutions which, while not hindering efficiency, permit a balanced development of our businesses, and equally permit full employment with the creation of new jobs. The Mondragon Cooperative Corporation assumes an historical responsibility which is concretized in its member cooperatives.

Hope versus Despair

When the Basques, along with other democrats, lost the war against the dictator Franco in 1939, the great threat was despair. The Mondragon founders recognized that the only way to conquer this despair was through hope in the strength of their values. While Franco and his friends had the economic, military and political power, the only thing left for the Basques was the wealth of their human resources. Instead of setting up businesses simply for the individual good of a small group at the top, they set out to work for the common good. There was no simple formula and there were no quick answers. There was mainly a reliance on the good to be found in all people.

Although Don José Maria was the teacher, leader and mentor for the Mondragon complex up until his death in 1976, the sources go beyond him as an individual. Dr. Alex Laidlaw, an international authority on cooperatives and a native of Cape Breton in Canada, pointed out the mistake of attributing the success of a movement to one or two individuals. Laidlaw was rooted in classical thought and he claimed that social economic movements would only be successful to the extent they were based on universal realities. He said that the great innovations in social economic reform were not so much the result of something new that a person created, but rather that a person discovered or rediscovered the deeper reality in the nature of society itself. The leaders in worthwhile social-economic movements, said Laidlaw in 1961, "were great and influential, not because of their personality or even their dedication, but basically because they were champions of eternal truth, truth which weary humanity all over the world is searching for."[1]

Alasdair MacIntyre, one of the leading British/American philosophers of our day, writes that modern empiricism has engendered a reductionist view of life. When the post-renaissance philosophers rejected Aristotle, they rejected too much. While admitting that much of Aristotle's physical science was primitive, he claims that the basic concept of human nature was accurate. MacIntyre agrees with Aristotle that there is more to being human than can be discovered by physical observation. When the human person is conceptualized in a mechanistic fashion, then it is easy to assume that all human needs can be met through technological tools.

In his view of human nature and society, MacIntyre is very close to what Don José Maria was talking about. The human world, for Aristotle and Judaeo-Christian thinkers, is similar. "Both are conceived as communities in which people in company pursue the human good and not merely as what the modern liberal state takes itself to be, providing the arena in which each individual seeks his or her private good."[2] The identity of a person is tied up with the common good, the group's purpose. Behind all of the Mondragon structures there is an underlying conception of the human person built on the notion of a common purpose and the common good.

B: THE TEN PRINCIPLES

While eminently pragmatic and effective in the market place, the importance of Mondragon's underlying values is always evident. In the long run, the direction of the complex will be determined by whatever group controls the philosophy. That power resides in the Congress. To date the Mondragon Congress has held to the basic values. For example, at the annual meeting of the Congress in 1987, the members agreed on a revised set of principles to serve as the goal and guideline for all members.[3] They include the basic principles of the International Cooperative Alliance but go further. They are as follows:

1. OPEN ADMISSION

The system is open to all who agree with the basic cooperative principles without regard to ethnic background, religion, political beliefs, or gender.

2. DEMOCRATIC ORGANIZATION

The cooperative system is based upon the equality of owner-workers. Aside from limited and special circumstances all workers must be members. The cooperative is democratically controlled on the basis of one member, one vote; its governing structures are democratically controlled and are also responsible to the general assembly or other elected bodies.

3. SOVEREIGNTY OF LABOUR

Labour is the essential transformative factor of society. The cooperatives renounce wage labour, give full power to the owner-workers to control the co-ops, give primacy to workers in the distribution of surpluses, and work to extend the cooperative choice to all members of society.

4. INSTRUMENTAL CHARACTER OF CAPITAL

Capital is basically accumulated labor and a necessary factor in business development and savings. The co-ops pay a just but limited return on capital saved or invested, a return that is not directly tied to the losses or surpluses of the co-ops. Their need for capital shall not impede the principle of open admission, but (after an initial trial period) co-op members must make a substantial, affordable and equal financial investment in the cooperative.

5. SELF-MANAGEMENT

Cooperation involves both collective effort and individual responsibility. Cooperation is the development of the individual not against others but with others. Democratic control means participation in management and the ongoing development of the skills needed for self-management (autogestion). There must be clear information available on the co-op's operations, systematic training of owner-workers, internal promotion for management positions, and consultations and negotiations with all cooperators in organizational decisions that affect them.

6. PAY SOLIDARITY

The co-ops will practice both internal and external pay solidarity. Internally, the total pay differential between the lowest-and the highest-paid member shall not exceed a factor of one to six. Wages should be comparable to those prevailing in neighbouring conventional firms.

7. GROUP COOP-ERATION

Co-ops are not isolated entities. Cooperation exists on three levels: among individual co-ops organized into groups; among co-op groups; and between the Mondragon system and other movements.

8. SOCIAL TRANSFORMATION

Cooperation in the Mondragon system is an instrument for social transformation. As Don José Maria Arrizmendiarrieta, founder of the movement, wrote, "Cooperation is the authentic integration of people in the economic and social process that shapes a new social order; the cooperators must make this objective extend to all those that hunger and thirst for justice in the working world."

The Mondragon co-ops reinvest the major portion of their surpluses in the Basque community. A significant portion goes toward new job development, to community development (through the use of social funds), to a social security system based on mutual solidarity and responsibility, to cooperation with other institutions (such as unions) advancing the cause of Basque workers, and to collaborative efforts to develop Basque language and culture.

9. UNIVERSAL NATURE

The co-ops proclaim their solidarity with all who labor for economic democracy, peace, justice, human dignity, and development in Europe and elsewhere, particularly with the peoples of the Third World.

10. EDUCATION

Education is essential for fulfilling the basic cooperative principles. It is fundamentally important to devote sufficient human and economic resources to cooperative education, professional training, and general education of young people for the future.

THE TEN PRINCIPLES

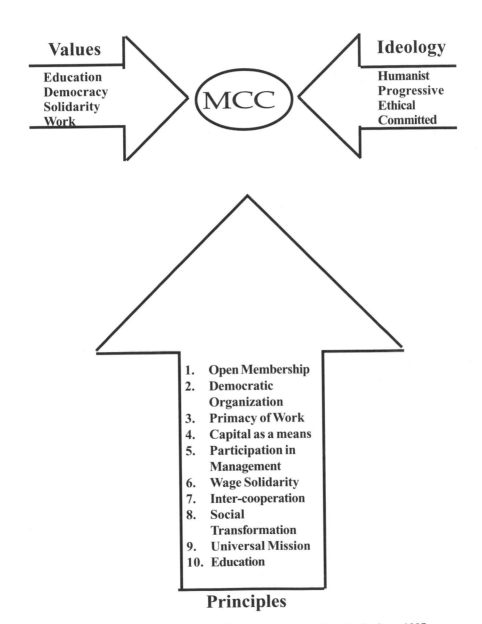

Values

Education
Democracy
Solidarity
Work

MCC

Ideology

Humanist
Progressive
Ethical
Committed

1. Open Membership
2. Democratic Organization
3. Primacy of Work
4. Capital as a means
5. Participation in Management
6. Wage Solidarity
7. Inter-cooperation
8. Social Transformation
9. Universal Mission
10. Education

Principles

Source: "Introducción a la Experiencia Cooperativa de Mondragón, Otalora, 1997

C: ENTERPRISE CREATION AND DEVELOPMENT

The sixth operating guideline attached to the Mondragon Mission Statement clearly points out the obligation to reinvest and expand to create jobs for those who do not have jobs. Conventional corporations and even many cooperatives are satisfied if their employees receive increased wages and the customers increased dividends. The Mondragon value system obliges the sucessful businesses to turn outwards instead of inwards. Azurmendi quotes a church document which influenced the early organizers:

> Above all you must recognize the danger of turning in on ourselves, which happens to cooperatives, enjoying the profits which previously belonged to the capitalists. This is corporate egoism, which englobes all the individual egoisms. The cooperative movement will necessarily feel this temptation.[4]

In this regard, Mondragon stands out and bears closer scrutiny. Not only has Mondragon started new enterprises; it has also kept them operational. When we recognize that more than half of all new businesses created in the United States are *expected* to fail in the first five years, we see that the question of maintenance is important. Besides avoiding bankruptcies, Mondragon has also managed to create new businesses in an increasingly competitive international economy. In this section the first question for examination concerns how Mondragon decision-makers were able to create new enterprises; the other question for discussion is just as important, namely how were they able to maintain those businesses when difficulties arose.

As implied in the basic Mission, new enterprise creation was of key concern from the beginning. Regardless of how successful one individual enterprise might be, the founders still considered it a moral responsibility to create new businesses as long as there were unemployed people in the Basque region. Such creation was possible with the growth of the Caja. Since the Caja accumulated more capital than was needed in existing enterprises, and since accumulating capital without a use didn't make much sense, expansion became an operating principle. Shortly after the Caja was set up, it was divided into two departments. One was the Banking Department, and the other was the Entrepreneurial Division. It became the responsibility of the Entrepreneurial Division to discover and promote new ideas for business.

The **Entrepreneurial Division**, which resembled a combined chartered accounting and technical consulting company, had a threefold function: 1) the development of new cooperative enterprises, 2) the provision of technical consulting assistance to members, and 3) the audit and monitoring of the financial operations of all member organizations in outside but conventional and secure investments. The Entrepreneurial Division became the support and nerve centre for the total Mondragon complex. The functions of development were divided into the six departments: Economic Analysis; Agroforestry; Urban Planning; Auditing; Intervention; and Industrial Promotion.

i) The Economic Analysis Department was designed to study national and international trends especially at the macro-economic level. At least five years before Spain entered the Common Market, this department had been analyzing and forecasting the positive impact upon their enterprises. While they issued regular reports on various aspects of the Basque economy, they also made periodic studies of the world economy to pinpoint four or five of the most dynamic areas in the international economy. This helped to focus research.

ii) Agroforestry: The Agricultural and Food Promotion Department provides the necessary technical and entrepreneurial assistance for the agroforestry area. In some older socialist traditions, we often see disparaging references to the "idiocy" of the countryside, an attitude which generated tension and opposition between the rural and the urban sectors. Mondragon leaders chose the rural over the urban as being supportive of a more communal mode of life. Thus they brought technology to agroforestry as well as to the heavy industries of urban centres.

iii) The Urban Planning Department plans such infrastructure as sewer, water and electrical systems as well as plans for buildings and structures such as industrial parks and shopping malls.

iv) The Auditing Department carries on a continual process of analyzing and informing. According to the terms of the Contract of Association, each cooperative enterprise must present a yearly budget as well as a monthly profit and loss statement. Each associated cooperative undergoes an obligatory audit every two years. All the financial information is analyzed with the help of a sophisticated computerized operating system. An attempt is made to avoid financial surprises. The Auditing Department also maintains profiles of enterprises in the traditional sector in order to make comparisons.

v) The Intervention Department which provides planning and management services, also specializes in helping out enterprises in difficulty. If the Auditing Department discovers a developing problem with the finances of one of the associated enterprises, an Intervention team will be organized to assist the local management. These are the trouble-shooters who try to prevent problems from getting worse.

vi) The Industrial Promotion Department is responsible for the initiation of new industrial cooperatives. As part of their continual process of product identification and feasibility, department members developed an international network with investigating agents in countries such as Japan, Germany, France and the USA. These agents gather once a year to discuss ideas for new product development. This department provides specialized services in fields such as production engineering, marketing, legal services and finance.

As with all the other cooperative enterprises, the cost of services provided by the Entrepreneurial Division is recovered on a fee-for-service basis. The usual yearly budget for these kinds of activities has been over five million dollars. Of this, 64 per cent is billed directly to the associate enterprises for services rendered. The other 36 per cent comes from the Caja as payment for a range of generic services such as the regular auditing of client-enterprises. As a policy the Caja yearly allocates a budget for the development of new enterprises. In 1987, the amount consisted of one dollar for every thousand dollars of assets.

The effects of integration and modern technology are striking. Conveyor belts link the Lenniz furniture factory to an adjacent sawmill. Timber arrives for milling, then passes next door into an ultra-modern factory system regulated by computer. Retail customers in department stores choose a model for their kitchen layout. The order is immediately transmitted to the factory which operates on a modular system, turning out, with the same machines, a wide variety in style and colour. Crates of furniture are automatically stacked at loading portals. When there is a sufficient load for a particular town or city then it is delivered. There is little inventory. All of this is a result of linking forest production to the retail market, using planning and technology.

In a typical month, the Division analyzes about thirty proposals. A filtering process serves to develop a short list so that about ten per cent (three) reach the second level. At a monthly meeting, perhaps one likely product is chosen for a preliminary feasibility study. This is a simple low cost testing of the markets and, whenever the indicators are positive, the process continues in a more intensive manner.

Before a full scale feasibility study is begun, two key people must be appointed. One is the advisor or the "godparent" and the other is the prospective manager. A search is made throughout the system for the most suitable managerial person who is then assigned to this project. If the feasibility study is positive, the implementation process begins. First, the Board of the Caja must approve the new product as worthy of financial support. Then the manager recruits an initial technical team from within the system and a new cooperative enterprise is incorporated. An example will help to clarify the process.

A few years ago a market opportunity in the field of forklifts was identified. After a positive feasibility study, a manufacturing license was purchased from Mitsubishi. A new cooperative was soon incorporated. In their usual cautious manner, the organizers began by assembling components purchased from Mitsubishi. If the enterprise was profitable they would manufacture the complete product. An advisor or godparent was assigned to monitor the company for two years on behalf of the department.

The cost of product development was approximately $60,000. Of this, the Basque government paid 40 per cent and the rest was assigned as a long term loan to the new enterprise. Thus the new company began with an initial debt of $36,000. This method of initial financing for new enterprises is very significant for community groups wondering how to start a business and where to find a "grant." If the group has confidence it can borrow and let the new enterprise pay it back.

In the case of the forklift company, Oinakar, $2.3 million was required to launch it into full operation. The necessary starting capital was amassed in the following manner. Approximately thirty-five workers constituted the membership and they contributed approximately $9,000 per worker for a capitalization $315,000. The Caja provided a $1.5 million loan, and the Basque government approximately $0.5 million. Sales for Oinakar in 1989 were approximately $6 million.

The criteria for approving a new venture are: 1) that a suitable manager can be found 2) that the investment per job does not exceed $100,000 (thus, an enterprise with 10 employees would not be approved if it required capital of over one million dollars) and 3) that by the fourth year there will be a financial break-even point. If there is not a break-even at that time then the venture will be changed or rejected.

It is important to note that the Mondragon structures are in constant evolution. The foregoing section describes the process and results as they existed in the early 1990s. Recently, some organizational changes have taken place. (Hence the apparent inconsistency in the use of past and present tense.) Nevertheless, the fundamental approach remains.

Role of Research

Research and Development permeates all of the Mondragon institutions. Connected with the Polytechnical University are a number of research institutes which play a key role not only in new enterprise development, but also in the maintenance of what they have. The three important centres are: Ikerlan, Ideko and Saiolan.

THE IKERLAN TECHNOLOGICAL RESEARCH CENTRE is an offshoot from the Polytechnical College. It began in 1974 with the Caja contributing the land, building and equipment while the College contributed researchers. Over the years researchers have developed prototypes, such as industrial robots, and CAD/CAM with their own model of a flexible manufacturing unit. With a staff of over one hundred, they are able to offer a wide range of technical skills that the individual enterprise could not afford. With a special orientation towards technology transfer they accept a wide variety of commissioned projects in the area of industrial instrumentation, computation and design, software and robotics. The method is to establish a mixed team comprised of Ikerlan staff and client-enterprise staff. Recently, *Ideko* was set up as a separate entity to specialize in production engineering.

SAIOLAN is one of the newer parts of the Mondragon consortium. It specializes in the creation of new enterprises which use high technology. It combines elements of business incubation with the development of young entrepreneurs. Based on their own experience they have evolved a unique approach which results in the creation of approximately three new businesses per year. The centre has a staff of 18 who dedicate 25% of their time to teaching and 75% to research and business development. They specialize in sifting through ideas and concepts that have some potential for implementation in their region. I will describe the process in sequence.

1. **Promotion:** They visit universities and organize workshops to explain their concept of business creation in the contemporary world. This is a quasi recruitment campaign.
2. **Selection of prospective entrepreneurs:** Saiolan advertises every year for applicants to compete for entrepreneur bursaries. Normally the applicants have a university degree in engineering or business but sometimes come from the workplace. In 1996, they received 300 applications from which they choose 12. It is interesting that academic marks are not the key consideration. They look for imagination, initiative and a sense of humour.
3. **Phase One:** The first three months is a formation programme where the students attend classes and are taught the basic concepts of modern business.

4. **Phase Two:** The students are broken up into teams of two or so and the second six months is spent in the study of a selected sector. A personal tutor is appointed for each student. The sector might be information technology, furniture manufacture, accounting services etc. The student must get to know the state of the art in that particular sector. After submitting a report, the student chooses a product or service in that sector and becomes a promoter.

5. **Phase Three.** This is the feasibility phase and lasts one and a half years. It involves a business plan covering market studies, technology plan, finance etc.
The promoter ends this phase by producing and selling a sample.

6. **Phase Four:** The promoter then must present the application to the affiliated bank (the Caja). Financial experts make a tough analysis. If the bank finally agrees, they will make an initial loan, at a reduced interest rate, of up to $100,000 per project. The promoter does not need collateral beyond his or her personal guarantee.

7. **Test period**- two years within the incubator context.

Most of the businesses created employ two to six persons. These vary in form from private incorporation, to co-operatives and joint ventures. Creation of two or three successful businesses per year is considered very successful. Sailon is funded mainly by the economic division of government with some investment from affiliated local businesses. Saiolan also earns money through special technical contracts with local businesses.

Overall Development Strategy

Leaders in the Mondragon Experiment speak in terms of a Strategic Triangle for Development with three components; technology, formation (a term which covers both education and training) and finance.

A. **Technology** is emphasized in every part of the system. The Mondragon goal is to use the best technology available in the world. The key institutional instruments, Saiolan and Ikerlan have the mission of maintaining the most up-to-date modern technology. As an indication of commitment to technological excellence, the FAGOR Group committed $18 million, which represents 3.25 per cent of their sales, to research and development in 1989.

B. **Formation** is assured through institutions such as Saiolan, the Technical College, Ikasbide (Management and Board

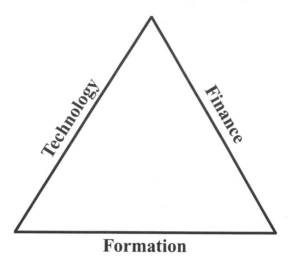

Formation

Training Centre) as well as the general employee formation program. Commitment to development of the workforce is manifested by the fact that the Congress decided
to allocate $600 per employee for the formation program.
This amounts to over $15 million for one year. Besides the
general formation programs, such as consumer education
throughout the system, Ikasbide has a variety of specialized programs. These cover everything from in-service
courses for marketing managers to educational weekends
for board members to learn balance-sheet interpretation.

C. **Finance** is assured through the Caja Laboral Popular. All
pension funds and worker capital accounts must be deposited in their own credit union. It is an exercise in capital
entrapment. With over one hundred branches concentrated
in the areas where their businesses are located, Mondragon
has promoted the idea, "Savings or Suitcases." Basques
like to live and work in their own area rather than pack
their suitcases and leave. With this motivation savings have
been high.

In observing the total system one is impressed by the variety of institutions which all seem to be mutually supporting. The triangle indicates
that any one element on its own is not adequate. Each is a necessary but
not a sufficient condition for success. The driving force seems to come
from the continual collaboration and systematic integration which creates
a tremendously powerful synergy.

D: PROVIDING FOR CONTINUANCE

Mondragon has measures in place to assure the future of both the individual in the organization and the future of the enterprises it has established.

Job Security. In an age of economic uncertainty, when many workers are now becoming more concerned with job security than with higher incomes, the system of Mondragon is very attractive. Although the Mondragon workers do not have a legal job guarantee, they do have a moral one and effective life-time job security. Through zone agreements, workers are able to move from factory to factory. Thus it can happen that in factory X there is the introduction of new technology such that the work formerly done by 100 workers will now be done by 50. Instead of fighting the change, the redundant workers are put on retraining and hired by other Mondragon factories in the same zone. When a factory requires more workers, the manager usually prefers to hire workers from the system because they are highly skilled. They carry with them a work culture that is based on collaboration and consensus rather than labour-management conflict.

Mondragon provides unemployment benefits (for downtime between job transfers) and medical service through a number of clinics. In 1982 an Insurance Division was added. The total social security system is based upon worker contributions with employees able to choose between a variety of levels which vary in price.

Enterprise Security. In the world of today, enterprise security is an issue related to job security. Every day the newspapers carry stories of bankrupt businesses. However, in the Mondragon system there have been no bankruptcies. When a company is in difficulty specialists from the Caja and the support groups analyze the situation. The problem may be that the company cannot keep up payments on the loans. Then the credit union may propose a solution that involves dropping the interest rate from 10% to 5%. The workers may be required to accept lower wages. New product development may also be required. Usually the solutions require compromise and contributions from all sides.

In North America, credit unions, cooperative and community corporations are all, supposedly, working towards the same goal of community improvement. However, they have not learned the Mondragon lesson of solidarity and cooperation between enterprises. Jack Quarter in his book, *The Canadian Social Economy*[5] points out that community-oriented businesses could have a tremendous power if they would ever decide to work together. However, in most cases they tend to work in isolation. Thus while so many in society are suffering from unemployment and poverty, this sleeping giant of social economic power is neutralized. By contrast, the Mondragon leaders realize the social-economic power and they use it.

As the nineties draw to a close, despair permeates and paralyzes many of our populations. Yet, so many still dream that some breakthrough in science and technology will save us all and provide the good life. For awhile, it was nuclear fission with its immense capacity to create cheap energy. We didn't realize the terrible unforeseen consequences. Now many people are dreaming of nuclear fusion as the answer. As Don José will point out, the solution is not outside of us in some new technology, it is inside of us, in our universal values. Unless we discover that, the needed technology will drive us and we will not be able to drive it. The secret is in the vision.

Notes

1. Laidlaw, "Focus on the Antigonish Movement," Address for the opening of new residence, Coady International Institute, N.S., October 17, 1961, p. 1.
2. Alisdair MacIntyre, *After Virtue*, London: Duckworth Press, 1981.
3. *Trabajo y Union, Lankide* (official magazine of MCC). All further references will be abbreviated to *TU Lankide,* May 1987, p. 4.
4. José Azurmendi, *El Hombre Cooperativo,* Mondragon, Spain: Caja Laboral Popular, 1984, p. 638. Translated by the author. Further references will be to Azurmendi.
5. Toronto: Lorimer, 1992
6. Cf. *TU Lankide*, April, 1996, p. 42.

CHAPTER 3

A NEW VISION

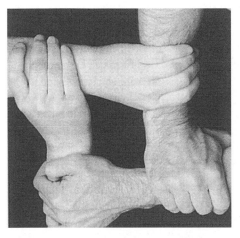

Visions do not occur in outer space or in the world of pure ideas. They grow in the minds of real people who live in a real world. Thus, before we can understand the Mondragon achievement, we must focus on Don José Maria Arrizmendiarrieta (1915-1976). As a young man, Don José Maria lived in a climate of intense debate over social reform. The Spanish Civil War (1936-1939), in which he participated, was the violent continuation of the debate about what kind of social order should exist in Spain. During his whole life Don José Maria's efforts were energized by a deep intention to help establish a new social order. This chapter discusses how he pursued this and what it meant to him.

First of all, Mondragon is the Spanish translation for the Basque word Arrasate. In the early 1940s the Madrid government insisted that the Basques use Spanish and not Basque in their placenames. This anomaly explains a lot about the ambivalence of being Basque in a nation dominated by the Spanish. Don José Maria was very conscious of the proud Basque tradition. The Basques have a language that is older than Gaelic and is not related to any other language in the world as far as anybody can tell. Historically the Romans were unable to defeat the Basques, who simply retreated into the mountains. However, in the twentieth century during the Spanish Civil War, the Basques joined the Republicans and were defeated by Franco and Hitler.

When the Civil War broke out in 1936, Don José Maria interrupted his studies for the priesthood to join the Basque army. While in the service, he became conscious of the fact that Hitler's command of the best technology in Europe enabled him to play a deciding role in the Spanish Civil War. The Nazi bombing of Guernica, portrayed by Picasso, had a profound and terrible meaning for the Basques. After narrowly escaping execution in one of Franco's prisoner-of-war camps, he was ordained a priest and sent to the village of Mondragon in the Basque heartland. As assistant-pastor in the local church, Don José Maria organized a technical school because he was convinced that the future of the world would be decided by whoever controlled the best technology.

The technical school, set up by Don José Maria in the 1940s, eventually grew to become the Polytechnical University, the source of training and research for present day Mondragon. Don José Maria organized study groups from among the students to discuss problems in the world. He assisted some of these students to pursue studies in engineering. The founders of ULGOR were some of the first engineering graduates. These five dedicated young men formed the core for all new business initiatives. Although Don José Maria held no formal position in the business complex, he continued to be their guiding light and mentor until his death.

Some of the pro-Franco, conservative Church leaders criticized him, but Don José Maria continued to promote the establishment of new economic structures as the only means for the Basque people to survive. He knew that they could not depend upon help from Madrid, the centre of political and economic power dominated by Franco. When the ULGOR company needed money, they set up their own bank asking the Basque people to use their capital for industry in the Basque region rather than in Madrid. The early motto of their community bank, "Savings or Suitcases," told a lot about the flight of capital and outmigration of the young.

Conscious that they could not rely on outside sources, Don José Maria and his team insisted that each new enterprise should remain a part of an economic whole. Not only individuals, but also these new businesses were asked to cooperate with each other. The Polytechnical University helped the new enterprises and the enterprises helped the Polytechnical University. Isolated they were weak but together they were strong. In 1988, echoing the thought of Don José Maria, Juan Leibar, the president of the Polytechnical University in Mondragon, in a lecture to a study tour, observed, "We Basques have used up all of our mineral resources and we have to sail thousands of miles for fish. Our only resources now are human ones, so education and technology are essential for our survival as a people."

When we read the writings of Don José Maria we find quite a number of cases where he changed his opinion. At one time he says that the proper place for a woman is in the home, and then later he says that women must learn to manage business corporations. This appears contradictory unless we understand his theory of knowledge. He believed that valid knowledge about the world could only be gained through involvement in worldly activity. Between practice and theory there is an ongoing dialectic: the theory affects the practice and the practice affects the theory. As Azurmendi puts it:

> Thought and action are intertwined in him in a dynamic inter-
> action of thought-action-thought, in which thought provokes
> action and action corrects and conditions the thought.[1]

Don José Maria held firmly to universal principles about moral behaviour in our social relations, but he was extremely opposed to dogmatic judgments about institutions in the world. His intellectual stand regarding the concrete, empirical order was a fluid and open one. Unquestionably, he considered ideas and intellectual reflection to be essential, but only if worthwhile action resulted; they are two sides of a single coin. If he proposed something and someone said that it could not be done, he would respond: "Let us try and see." He himself learned through practice. Thus later in life, he sometimes adopted positions that he had earlier opposed.

There are at least three instances where Don José Maria changed his position as a result of his experience. The first, already cited above, concerns women. Earlier, he spoke very strongly about a woman's place being in the home. Later, he said that with modern domestic conveniences there was no real necessity for women to remain at home. He became angry when he heard of a mother discouraging her daughter from reading a newspaper because it was inappropriate for a woman. Even later he said that the business corporation is the building block of society and women are needed therein. Furthermore, he promoted special structures to allow women a chance to develop without male dominance. He claimed that women would be especially effective in the new cooperative corporations once their domestic skills were transformed into business skills.

The second case concerns the structure of society. At one time he agreed with the generally accepted opinion that the family was the basic unit of society. In later years, he claimed that the business corporation was the unit or building block of society. He opined that in the modern age, whether we like it or not, the world of business is predominant in moulding the fabric of society not only on the economic level, but also on the social, political, and cultural levels and perhaps even on the spiritual level. It is interesting to note that Don José Maria read the writings of Herbert Marcuse who argued that American industry was shaping family and social life through television advertising. His reading reinforced observation from his own involvement in the world of industry. He found that those who still held that the family is the unit of society were really expressing their hopes and wishes and not the lived reality. Here again, Don José Maria elected to respond to the world as it actually is but with a view to changing it to a "new order."

The third example of experience causing Don José Maria to change his ideas concerns the notion of truth. In his early years he attacked liberalism for having abandoned a sense of absolute truth. Later on, he said that truth is not absolute, that it evolves in practice. Of course, the term "truth" is a very ambiguous one. He recognized that sometimes it concerns factual statements about the concrete world; at other times it refers to abiding values which transcend historical circumstances. For instance, the value of motherhood is absolute and universal while the factual circumstances of how motherhood is exercised changes with the facts of history and context. Don José Maria was able to distinguish between what was essential and primary and what was secondary and changing. *(See the reference to Alasdair McIntyre in Chapter 2.)*

However, Don José Maria thought the analysis and debate of ideas were essential tools to prevent values from becoming sterile "isms." "Ideas divide us but necessity unites us" was a phrase often repeated by Don José Maria. He objected strongly to those who acted out of loyalty to ideas or to "isms." He explicitly rejected Marxism, Communism, Socialism, Capitalism, and even Cooperativism. He even tended to reduce to a minimum the dogmas of religion; thus he was in no way prepared to accept the dogmas of the many "isms" which paraded as absolute truths.

Social action itself was not exempt from debate and development of its principles. "In the first place, concerning social action, I would like to say that I do not conceive it as something that can be encapsulated within the narrow confines of a formula and as formulas conceived a priori."[2]

Oftentimes people propose a theory or formula for social action, and complain that it doesn't work. They say things like: "It ought to work," and, "It would work, if politicians weren't so dishonest and people weren't so lazy." This is not untypical, especially of theoreticians in economics. Don José Maria would accuse them of operating in a hypothetical world instead of the real world. He claimed that one could not know the real world in a laboratory; it can only be known in doing concrete actions.

A very good illustration of his approach concerns the question as to whether a humanistic cooperative business corporation can continue in a capitalist society. Key thinkers in the Personalist tradition such as Mounier, an early twentieth-century French philosopher, claimed that a business institution based on personal values could only survive in a non-capitalist society based upon similar values. Don José Maria challenged this. For him this kind of question can only be decided through testing the idea in practice.

Although he was a disciple of personalists such as Mounier, he considered this sort of position idealist and unfounded. It often became an excuse for inaction. So, in spite of armchair socialists who accused him of band-aid tactics, he established cooperatives in a capitalist society. Because of this, some people call him a realist.

Facing reality and changing it for the better are both essential to Don José Maria's approach If things are going to change, he pleaded, we have to act in the world we have, not the one we dream of. But he admonished that it is not enough to understand the world; we must change it. Of course this methodological rule of relating theory to practice is not original. In the Judaeo-Christian tradition there is a strong element demanding that faith be related to "works." Of the early Christians it was said "By their fruits ye shall know them." The first cooperative in Europe was set up by a small Christian group in Paris in the early 19th century. The kibbutzim of Israel are a striking example of concretized religious values.

Don José Maria's decision to dedicate himself to the building of a new practical social order is rooted in four traditions: 1) the social doctrine of the Church, 2) the Basque social tradition, 3) the epistemology of socialism, and 4) the philosophy of personalism.

A: SOURCES

The Church Tradition. At one end of the spectrum of attitudes towards the social order is the view some people take of religion as a system which enables them to survive various temptations and tribulations in life and thereby reach the heavenly "kingdom" when they die and attain their eternal reward. (Pie in the sky when you die.) At the other end are the people who take religion as a way of life by which society is transformed into a new kingdom here on earth. In response to these extreme religious positions, various popes have written encyclicals outlining what is now called the social doctrine of the Church.

Although Don José Maria eventually came to the conclusion that this social doctrine was too general and abstract to be useful in practice, he was deeply influenced by it, especially through the Christian Worker Movement. This movement was particularly strong in Belgium and France during the 1940s and 50s. Young workers formed study-groups in various factories in an attempt to relate the teachings of religion to the work-place.

The guiding motto of the Christian Worker Movement was "See, Judge, Act." Rather than performing as a passive mechanical tool in industry, the young worker was encouraged to take responsibility in the transformation of industry. Thus, instead of merely being a necessary burden to earn money, work could become an opportunity for personal growth and a social contribution to the general society.

Interestingly enough, Pope John Paul II, like Don José Maria, was also a disciple of Emmanuel Mounier and he wrote a social encyclical on work called *Laborem Exercens*.[3] In this latter encyclical, the Pope develops some of the older themes of the social encyclicals. He explicitly rejects capitalism and communism. He makes radical claims that everyone has the right to a job, and if the state cannot provide a job, then the state has the moral duty to provide unemployment insurance. He makes explicit the earlier Church position on "work" saying that workers cannot be the "object" of capital, but must be allowed to function at work in a manner that will develop all their personal capacities. An obvious way to develop personal decision-making capacities is to give workers a share in management.

The longstanding tradition within the Church of viewing the economy as a means for more profound human purposes has come to expression in various concrete ways. As long ago as the *Acts of the Apostles*, a new communal society is described as the norm. (The kibbutzim of Israel go back to an even more ancient source.) In the sixteenth century Thomas More describes a communal society without money in *Utopia*. The story of the Jesuit attempt to establish a campesino-controlled economy in Paraguay during the seventeenth century has been popularized in the movie *The Mission*.

During the nineteenth century, Church leaders had great difficulty coming to terms with the two contending traditions of communism and capitalism. At the end of the nineteenth century, Pope Leo XIII made the first major move to accept the positive elements of Marxism through his encyclical *Rerum Novarum (Of New Things)*. Catholic leaders in the co-operative and labour movements frequently referred to this encyclical. After attacking communism during the twentieth century, the Catholic Church is only now beginning to address the deep contradictions within capitalism. While the papal encyclicals cautiously address abuses of capitalism, liberation theologians challenge the foundation of capitalism itself.

Obviously Don José Maria was familiar with the rich tradition of social criticism throughout the Judaeo-Christian tradition. Besides the writers and activists in the Roman Catholic stream, most of the major denominations such as the Anglican, United and Presbyterian Churches have been active in addressing current social economic injustices. In North America social criticism flowered as the "social gospel," which finds radical expression in the Mennonite and Hutterite communities.

The Basque Social Tradition is rooted in their ancient history. The Basque people have lived in the same region for thousands of years and have never yielded to the disintegrating forces that have broken down other ancient European cultures such as the Celts. Basque social cohesion and the tenacity by which they have held on to their unique language is well known. Don José Maria, aware of a number of characteristics that enabled the Basques to survive, articulated them into the basic principles of the Basque cooperative movement. One was solidarity. That they have survived so many attacks, of a military, political, and cultural nature is argument enough that Basque solidarity plays a crucial role in their society. A visit to Guernica, their national shrine, makes that spirit very evident.

The other Basque characteristic identified by Don José Maria is hard work. He claims that, besides their solidarity, Basques have been able to survive only through hard work: a thousand years ago in their mines, then in the fishing fleets that went as far as Newfoundland and the east coast of North America. Thus he named their bulletin *TU (Trabajo y Union,* which in English would read *Work and Unity)*. His vision of a worthwhile human society is one characterized by the virtues of survival: solidarity and work.

The 1920s and 1930s saw very strong movements promoting socialism within the Basque region. Secular groups within the general society as well as Church groups articulated positions in favour of a more democratic society and a more just social economic system. The Basque region was massively in favour of the Republic in opposition to Franco's dictatorship. Don José Maria referred frequently to Basque writers concerning the theory of the cooperative movement as an instrument for popular emancipation.

Socialism: The third source of a new practical social order was socialism. Having been a student during the 30s, and a writer for an army magazine during the war, he was inevitably required to be knowledgeable concerning socialist theory. From such thinkers as Marx and contemporary French writer, St. Simon, he took some points and rejected others. For instance he retained notions concerning the fundamental role of workers in bringing about social-economic reform. In developing his own particular brand of socialism, he called for a "new order." He opposed state socialism, charging that in capitalism, capital held the power over the worker, while in state socialism, the state bureaucracy held the power over the worker. Also, he opposed violent revolution saying that a system put in place through force would always require force to maintain it.

In his view cooperativism was in no way opposed to the labour movement. He considered that the new order would be brought about through the collaboration of forces on three fronts: 1) the labour-union movement, 2) the cooperative movement, and 3) progressive political movements.

Personalism. Personalist thinkers such as Mounier and Maritain had an important influence on Don José Maria. These thinkers opposed capitalism as being hostile to personalist values, but they also opposed large, state centralized systems as being bureaucratic and impersonal. They praised the cooperative formula as an eminently appropriate mode of organizing business, because it allowed the participants to use their human qualities at work.

B: DON JOSÉ MARIA'S SYNTHESIS

Don José Maria's synthesis expressed frustration at the seeming opposition between the desire for personal development and the necessity for efficient production. From his vantage point in economically depressed Spain, the accomplishments of capitalistic Northern Europe were to be admired. Also he was critical of the dominant Spanish attitude towards work as somewhat of a divine punishment to be avoided. On the contrary he credits the Basque spirit of hard work as a major reason for their survival as a distinct.

Don José Maria Arrizmendiarrieta (1915-1976)

In the medieval Christian tradition, work was a burden and punishment; humans were to earn their bread by the sweat of the brow.[4] Work was viewed as a means of acquiring a ticket to pleasure and consumption. The nobility considered it beneath their dignity to be obliged to work. In Castile during the high Middle Ages the majority of the inhabitants being nobles of one sort or another, the region produced little and was relatively poor. In contrast, the Basque land and Catalonia, with far fewer nobles, developed the tradition and culture of artisanship and more people participated in the work force.

Don José Maria interpreted Calvin and related thinkers as viewing work in a positive way with their emphasis on work as a means of creating wealth rather than as a means to permit further consumption. When the result of work is reinvested for further work, work becomes something worthwhile in itself. While Don José Maria took up this positive notion of work, he disagreed with the individualistic sense of this tradition. He saw the act of work as being a collective one. Each individual depends upon others in order to be able to perform the act of work. No one individual can claim to be completely self-made, as is often portrayed in modern business circles. Besides the dependency on God, the individual depends on a vast array of support, from family to school, to government, to neighbourhood and so on. In classical thinking, since the act of work is due to society, so also the wealth created by work is fundamentally due to society.

Don José Maria saw the contradiction between the sense of work as the means to increase personal consumption versus the view of work as communal resource building by creating wealth. He also saw the contradiction between the view that the shape of society is determined by economic structures as opposed to the traditional view that all is determined by good moral attitudes. He attempted to take what was acceptable in both positions and thus achieve a workable synthesis. He said: "The economic revolution will be moral or it will not succeed...the moral revolution will be economic or it will not succeed."[5] Thus goodwill and intentions are important but they are not enough. Efficient business structures are also a fundamental necessity.

Aranguren[6] says that Don José Maria was a precursor of the utopian movements of the 1960s. He was opposed to the depersonalization involved in capitalistic economic development. He sought to conciliate both the economic imperative and the moral imperative. In the personalist tradition, Don José Maria took morality in the sense of self-creation. Thus any structures created from his theories had to allow for this to happen.

Morality involves persons taking responsibility for their own development and evaluating that development in terms of their own ideals. Goodness and badness consist in creating oneself in a good or bad manner, that is, a development of one's innate capacities or a distortion of those same capacities. "Morality" in this sense is unique to humans in that the human is the only animal who is the result of actions chosen freely and in collaboration with others. Granted there is increasing evidence that animals share and collaborate; but this is usually taken as a result of instinct and not a result of reflection and choosing.

Although the concept of choosing one's direction seems essential to any notion of morality, the Western tradition does not regard that power of choice as completely arbitrary. Jews, Christians and Moslems hold that we have a moral obligation to share the goods of the earth with our neighbour. In general they see this as an objective obligation inscribed in Nature itself. We are "free" to reject it, but we thereby do moral wrong.

Some of the statements of playwright Vaclav Havel, who became President of Czechoslovakia in 1989, are similar to the line taken by Don José Maria. For example Havel sees economic problems in spiritual terms. Conventional economists and politicians became confused when Havel referred to the problem of Europe as being spiritual. In his address to the joint session of Congress in Washington he declared that the members would have to put morality ahead of politics. As Ottawa, Washington and Berlin strive to become as productive as Tokyo, Havel struggles to make Prague into what he calls the "spiritual centre" of Europe.

Back in the 1960s Don José Maria had foreseen the frustration that would come from the Soviet model which neglected the personal and spiritual. He recognized that the activity which occupies most of a person's time and energy is work. Thus if human and moral development does not take place through work, it will not take place at all, or only minimally. If the producer-person and the moral-person are to be reconciled, then it will have to take place in the work situation. Both state socialism and private capitalism are deficient as models for human and social development. For example the Soviet model would assure protection of the common good through state enterprises but would deprive individuals of real input and control over their immediate situation; personal motivation and involvement disappear. Private capitalists produce efficiently but do so for their own selfish ends and to the detriment of the common good.

While agreeing with the socialist establishment that there is a hidden economic structure which affects change, Don José Maria held that there was also an underlying moral structure that was more basic and that dealt with deeper human needs and more powerful human possibilities.

The challenge was to build a society that avoided the dichotomy of complete state control in a materialistic economic system or a state of free individuals involved in selfish and competitive capitalism. Don José Maria looked for efficient methods to tap the creativity of individuals so that they, as persons, could develop and yet produce to fulfil their responsibility to the rest of society. The ideal model of the commercial corporation must therefore be efficient and productive for the public good and yet operate humanistically so that the work experience helps the worker develop in a positive way. The result of this dialectical tension and contradiction is a positive synthesis creating individual and social progress.

Approaches to Work

A narrow view of economics in the style of Milton Friedman results in a reductionist approach to work such that the only value of work is the product produced and this value is measured in monetary terms.[7] In the Judaeo-Christian view espoused by Don José Maria, work is an act that develops the person on many levels. On one level, participation in a creative process confers on the worker the dignity of being part of something bigger. The worker becomes more of a person by actualizing inner potentials. As a person, the worker has not only mechanical abilities but intellectual and moral capacities. While the mechanical is exercised through manipulation of machines, the intellectual and moral is exercised through participation in governance of the enterprise. Another level is the social. Through the workplace the worker plays a role with other workers and with the larger society. According to Aristotle, the person is a "political animal" and can only become fully human through participation in social groups. In classical thinking the isolated individual becomes dehumanized. In this tradition, from which Don José Maria comes, even the desert hermit, in speaking to God, must do so on behalf of all humankind. An excellent statement of this tradition is the encyclical on work by Pope John Paul (*Laborem Exercens*).

Karl Marx also criticized the dehumanizing effect of industrial age work and admired the personal involvement of the medieval craftsperson. For him work was the only means of personal growth. As Don José Maria noted, the Soviet system exaggerated this insight so that work became an oppressive ideal, with feasts as "glorious" work-days. As opposed to this, in the classical view, leisure is the natural culmination of work; it is the time when people can relax and enjoy the fruits of their labour. In this view, the reduction of obligatory work hours is positive because leisure activities are as social and communitarian as work itself. The point is that authentic work adds to creation. We can add to creation not only in the production of commercial consumer goods, but also in the production of art, like music or poetry, and social activity which is done "for fun" and not for money.

Later in his life Don José Maria insisted that the tendency to value people only as producers of market goods could imply that the unemployed, the handicapped and retirees have no value whatever. Don José Maria warned against over-emphasizing any one aspect of life. Because of his appreciation for technology and worker education Don José Maria founded the technical school but yet he saw the dangers. "A professional school that is not, at the same time, a school for total human development, is digging its own grave."[8]

Dreams And Visions

Down through history people have had visions about a new way of living together in society: Socrates, Christ, Thomas More, Calvin, St. Simon, Marx, Robert Owen and countless numbers during this century. But rare are the visions that are translated into real life change. Definitely, Don José Maria had a vision of a new kind of society. His writings go far beyond "creating jobs." The idea of society as atomistic individuals competing with each other was foreign to him. Also, the concept of "the social man" or the "historical man" where the individual person becomes merged in a greater social reality was alien to him. To find a middle course in the real world is indeed difficult, but that is what Don José Maria was trying to do. And to find such a middle course in the world meant embracing the impact of economics. An appropriate term to describe his approach would be "person centered economics."

The word "economics" from the original Greek means "management of the household." This is a more classical notion of economics as distinguished from the number-crunching of so many modern economists. Household here means the space or place where we live as a group, so that we can replace "household" with "community." Then economics becomes community management. In this sense Don José Maria was an economist, not a passive economist but a proactive one. He had a vision of the community and set out as a manager to put it into practice.

Rare are the visionaries who can help make their visions become real-world experiments. The progressive Jesuits built wonderful farms in Paraguay; the ideas of thinkers such as Martin Buber inspired the kibbutzim of Israel and of course we have the Mennonites. Mondragon is rare in the world of today in that it is a secular complex fitting in and playing the economic game even though the vision of its leaders is different from the Friedmanites. As will become more apparent, Don José Maria was different from most visionaries of this century in that he combined social and moral insights with a deep appreciation of technology.

Ursula Franklin warns of the tremendous power of technology to impose compliance to its impersonal needs.[9] She challenges the commonly accepted notion that whatever is more efficient must be done. As a scientist she respects technology but sees it in the real world as a dehumanizing force that has gotten beyond the control of human purpose. This is especially so when technology becomes an instrument of the blind forces of the free market system. The reality of today's world order, where communities and cultures are being destroyed in the name of technology-driven economic progress, stands in stark contrast to the Mondragon vision of technology at the service of a person centred economic system.

Notes

1. Azurmendi, p. 727.
2. Don José Maria Arrizmendiarrieta, Vol. 1 ed. Mendizabal, p. 149. The Archival material containing all the writings and talks of Don José Maria are available at the Beaton Institute at the University College of Cape Breton. Quotations are translated from the Spanish by the author. All further references to this archival material will be under the rubric *DJM* with volume and page, are one of two Folios: CLP and FC.
3. Rome, 1981.
4. *Leisure, the Basis of Culture*, Josef Pieper, London, Fober and Fauer, 1952, p. 96.
5. *DJM*, vol. 1, p. 156.
6. José Luis L. Aranjuren, "Conceptions of the Economic and Moral Life," *TU Lankide,* Dec. 1989.
7. Milton Friedman, *Capitalism and Freedom*, Chicago: University of Chicago Press, 1962.
8. *DJM*, vol.1, p. 180.
9. Ursula Franklin, *The Real World of Technology* (The Massey Lectures) Toronto: CBC Enterprises, 1991.

CHAPTER 4

A CRITIQUE OF CAPITALIST, SOCIAL AND STATE ENTERPRISE

Before we can fairly consider the achievement in putting Mondragon legs on Don José Maria's ideas, we need to review the possibilities he had before him and his precise understanding of the components of available models.

Don José Maria distinguished among three models according to which the business corporation could be structured: 1) capitalist, 2) Soviet, and 3) communal. He had serious criticisms of both the capitalist and the contemporary Soviet models and some criticisms of traditional cooperative forms of business. His communal or cooperative model arose out of his criticism of the capitalist and Soviet models and in a sense could be considered a synthesis of them. Concerning previous communal models, he accepted some aspects and rejected others. An understanding of Don José Maria's criticism of the models available for his scrutiny is necessary to understand the full weight of the new cooperative model which he proposed.

Business Corporation. First, we must clarify what Don José Maria meant by a "business corporation" or a "business enterprise." The Spanish word *empresa* is used frequently in his writings. Some may translate this word as meaning simply enterprise, but from the context he clearly meant more than that. His definition is quite precise:

> The production of goods and services useful for the satisfaction of human needs is realized regularly by executing plans conceived and projected by persons or institutions through the mediation of an organization which makes viable the personal and economic collaboration of those agreeing to the convoca-

tion and option implied in such an initiative. We will call such an organization a business corporation.[1]

In other words, a corporation is a group of people acting as one through a systematic organization of their intentional efforts to produce what society needs. They achieve through the organized group what they cannot achieve as individuals.

This concept of a corporation contrasts with various other perceived interpretations. For some, the corporation means a **juridical reality** that regulates certain human activities in the pursuit of an intentional goal. For others, the corporation means an **economic entity** which is to be understood within an economic context, subject only to economic law. This is the tradition of "laissez faire" economics which took the blind forces of supply and demand for its guide. One of the best known defenders of this "free enterprise" view is Milton Friedman of the University of Chicago. In a criticism of those calling for corporate social responsibility, he says:

> This shows a fundamental misconception of the character and nature of a free economy. In such an economy there is one and only one social responsibility of business - to use its resources and engage in activities designed *to increase its profits* so long as it stays within the rules of the game, which is to say, engages in open and free competition without deception or fraud.[2]

For Don José Maria, the *empresa* or corporation is not just an economic or juridical reality but above all a **social reality.** The corporation, like so many institutions, is a social entity, that is, a union of people; more concretely, the corporation is a union of human conduct operating in pursuit of a common goal. The goal is fundamentally economic, and it requires juridical norms in order to function, but the purpose is strongly communitarian.[3] Clearly *empresa* in this context is more than what is conveyed by the English word "enterprise"; one person can constitute an enterprise but not a corporation.

A: CAPITALIST CORPORATION

For the capitalist, the corporation is a centre of production, the purpose of which is the acquisition of an optimum profit for the owners. Social improvement is a side-effect or a byproduct. Don José Maria admits that the capitalist corporation has improved in this generation, but this is less through any internal reform on the part of managers and stockholders than a result of external causes. Traditional corporations have been forced to change through pressures from labour unions and democratically elected governments. The thesis of Don José Maria is that the modern business corporation, as we know it, is fundamentally flawed and inappropriate as an institution and thus functions inadequately as the fundamental building block of society.

While admitting that the conditions of the typical worker had improved, Don José Maria still held that workers are treated as objects of capital always subject to the corporate purpose of increasing profits. The effects of such treatments are twofold. The first is at the individual level, where the worker is not given the opportunity to exercise personal capacities through some measure of control over the work process. The second is at the level of the community where whole regions (such as the Basque province) are allowed to deteriorate because of the external control of capital. North Americans should be sensitive to this criticism in the wake of the disasters caused by large multinationals closing down branch plants and causing terrible unemployment in so many places.

External Control. Control over production has long been a problem in the theory of corporate business. The great apostle of liberal economics, Adam Smith himself, opposed the formation of corporations when it involved absentee control. He favoured individually owned businesses and criticized outsider corporations because of the difficulty in ascribing responsibility when the resulting impact of decisions was distant from the corporate centre of control. He promoted individual responsibility and felt that a dispersed group of decision makers could hardly maintain responsibility for the results of their decisions.

Atlantic Canada, like so many other parts of the older industrial world, has suffered particularly from absentee ownership. The classical pattern involved outside investors buying the rights to primary Atlantic resources such as minerals and forests. They would make profits from these commercial operations and then use the profits for investment in other areas such as central Canada, Britain or the United States. The cost of generating this new capital was a great deal of suffering in the coal mines and forests of Atlantic Canada. The gains were short term and in favour of the owners in England or Montreal. Atlantic citizens of today experience the long-term results in ongoing unemployment and economic decline.

For Don José Maria the external control of Basque industry was clearly negative in its effects and had to be reformed.

Technology and Management

In addition to the above rather standard criticisms of capitalism by the socialist tradition there is another that bears elucidation. It has arisen precisely because of modern technology. This criticism concerns the factors of production. Traditional analysts talked about two factors of production and debated whether surplus value came from labour or capital. Don José Maria observed that in reality there are three factors of production: capital, labour and *management*. Control no longer rests with the stockholder owners but with management.

Don José Maria viewed management as an important and real factor of production, at least in highly technological industries. For him, the role of maintaining technological excellence falls within the sphere of management. The role of managing technology is a critical control function.

Because of his sensitivity to the role of technology, Don José Maria used the term "management" in a somewhat different sense than many business writers. Although he fails to explain it very well, he connects it closely to an appreciation of the importance of modern science and technology. On the one hand he views the manager as part of the work-force. This is indicated by the fact that the salary of the manager at Mondragon is determined in exactly the same manner as that of the most junior worker-member: by the ratio system, thus putting management in the same category as workers.

Nevertheless, when it comes to decision-making, the manager is placed in a special category. Don José Maria compares the top manager to a brain surgeon. It takes many years of study and training to produce a qualified brain surgeon. Because of this, the brain surgeon is able to make split-second decisions upon which people's lives depend. It would be ridiculous to organize the operating team into a committee and force the surgeon to seek consensus. As with the training of a brain surgeon, it takes years and years to prepare a manager to be able to handle the complex decisions of a large company in the post-industrial world. In Don José Maria's view, the success or failure of a modern business often depends upon the technological competence of management. Regardless of the good will and hard work of the general workforce, the business will flounder if management is not competent.

In other words, Don José Maria disagreed with the management theories of Mao Tse Tung, which stated that all decisions could be improved through the participation of workers. During the Chinese Cultural Revolution, scientists and intellectuals were sent to the villages to work as peasants. In the factories managers were required to submit decisions to committees of workers chosen from the factory floor. Neither the peasants nor the worker-committees had the competence to make the necessary decisions.

For Don José Maria, many of the new worker cooperatives in Europe could not succeed in a modern economy because they emphasized democratic decision-making to the detriment of an efficient decision-making system. The comments of Don José Maria concerning the fundamental importance of technology and of management reveal that he saw the role of management as having evolved. **Instead of managing people and money, it seems that management has a more important and challenging role: to manage technology and not be managed by technology itself.** According to Don José Maria, Karl Marx did not foresee this new danger inherent in technology and the technological business corporation.

Indeed, he saw an inevitable decline in traditional corporations because of their approach to management and technology. [4] Don José Maria believed that traditional corporations lack the flexibility to keep up with the changing demands of modern technology. The overriding intention to increase profits detracts from attention to quality. Although corporations claim in their publicity that quality is their first concern, their internal dynamism works against it. The exception may be in the case of Japan (in which Don José Maria had a special interest). [5]

Capitalist Corporations in Flux

During the 1980s, ten years after Don José Maria made his criticisms, many American writers were admitting some of the shortcomings of the traditional management role. As a result a number of fascinating changes have been taking place in the structure of large corporations. In the USA there has been a trend to disperse shares throughout a large segment of the population. Employee stock ownership plans (ESOPs) are now quite common in the United States. Over ten million workers own shares in their companies, although it is doubtful whether they have much control. However, there are very progressive examples, such as United Air Lines and Algoma Steel where employees do have control.[6] In Britain there has been a campaign to privatize crown corporations and spread the shares throughout the population. In 1986, corporation shares were held by over 20 per cent of the adult British population. Obviously, with the greater dispersion of ownership, management gains greater control. In the face of a wave of mergers and sometimes hostile takeover bids through "junk bonds" by financial speculators, there is a new development whereby managers are buying controlling blocks of shares.

These developments simply accentuate the basic question about control of the corporation. Should control belong to the shareholders through capital, should it belong to the managers, the government, the workers or the local community? Many questions are being asked. The whole corporate complex is in flux with all sorts of experimentation going on regarding shared management, worker profit sharing and other arrangements.

Juridical Aspects of the Traditional Corporation

Modern commentators tend to agree in their criticism of the new and radical separation between ownership and control in the large multinational corporations. In 1931 Berle and Means did a major analysis of the modern American corporation.[7] In 1981 the Twentieth Century Fund commissioned economist Edward Herman to re-appraise this study. Concerning the question of who controls the corporation he writes:

> Although subject to a great deal of criticism from 1932 up to the present on the score of method, inferences and policy conclusions, the central theme of *The Modern Corporation And Private Property*—that ownership and control in large corporations have been separated, with effective discretionary power in the hands of the active management rather than the stockholders—has become part of the conventional wisdom, accepted by conservatives like H.G. Manne, liberals like R.A. Gordon and J.K. Galbraith, and even Marxists like Paul A. Baran and Paul M. Sweezy. [8]

L.C.B. Gower is one of the most respected commentators on company law both in Britain and America. A number of law schools such as Dalhousie have used his book on company law as a text for many years. Gower calls for a reform of company law because the juridical structures do not reflect the corporate reality which exists today. He points out that at one time, a "corporation" or "company...implied an association of a number of persons for a common object, that object normally being the economic gain of its members." However, through the evolution of corporations, the association in a common endeavour no longer has a reality in most cases and is a mere legal fiction. "The running of the business is left to the directors, or probably to the managing directors, and the shareholder, although a member, is, in economic reality, but not in the eyes of the law, a mere lender of capital, on which he hopes for a return but without any effective control over the borrower." [9]

Peter Drucker, a well-known business writer at Claremont University in United States, makes some surprising observations such as: "The mega-state has all but destroyed citizenship. To restore it, the post capitalist polity needs a 'third sector', in addition to the two generally recognized ones, the 'private sector' of business and the 'public sector' of government. It needs an autonomous social sector." [10] These are not unusual statements for critical thinkers, but they are unusual for an establishment-type writer like Drucker. Don José Maria would be surprised at the number of leading thinkers who would support many of his ideas twenty years after his death.

A Prediction about Traditional Corporations

The Mondragon founder believed that there is a definite historical trend which will force the traditional corporations to disappear if they cannot conform to the new context. He discussed such trends in two senses. On one level he means a cultural development among working people. Ordinary working people are becoming more informed and educated, and therefore not so ready to accept blindly the results of corporate decisions. At a broader level, as the community becomes more articulate, there will be a more obvious gap between what the community desires and what the traditional profit-making corporation desires.[11] In other words there will be a clash of intentions. For instance, a large corporation may decide to close a branch in Yorkshire, Newfoundland or Maine as part of its corporate intention to cut costs. The intentions of the local people will obviously clash with the corporate intention. To the extent that corporations depend upon political will, then some of them will be forced out of existence.

Admittedly, Don José Maria was somewhat optimistic about the development of an informed public opinion. Other writers like Herbert Marcuse were not so optimistic, especially in light of the development of powerful psychological tools such as television. [12] However, Don José Maria claimed that even when the popular political will does not become sufficiently informed to demand change, many of the traditional European firms will collapse simply from their internal weakness. This was partially borne out during the 1970s and 1980s when so many Spanish firms went bankrupt. At the same time, Japanese firms, which he saw as being advanced in technology management, were flourishing. A reform of the capitalist model is necessary because its current structure is incapable of satisfactorily resolving a multitude of human, moral and economic problems. [13]

B: TRADITIONAL COOPERATIVES

Obviously Don José Maria was attracted to the cooperative model because, instead of giving the controlling votes to capital, it gave the control to persons through the mechanism of one vote per person. Also the personalist tradition to which he belonged favoured the cooperative model. However, he expressed strong reservations about cooperative businesses as they existed in practice.

Don José Maria held that a cooperative could not be defined simply according to its juridical structure. "Cooperativism is a complex of principles rather than a concrete structure." [14] What was required was a certain spirit and an intention to reform modern post-industrial society. He considered the institutional form to be relative and secondary; what is important is the purpose. Because of this he called upon cooperators to abandon structures and traditions whenever the good of the workers or the community required it. He endorsed the principles of the International Cooperative Alliance which allowed for a great deal of flexibility in the way concrete institutions were formed.[15] He observed that the European cooperatives did not appear to have the flexibility and technical capacity to play a leading role in society.[16] He considered that many of the cooperatives had become victims of dogmatism, especially regarding the use of capital.

Although Don José Maria openly opposed the capitalist system, he did not oppose the use of capital. It was especially in this regard that he found the traditional cooperatives to be weak. In order to function in modern society cooperatives need modern technology, and this in turn requires huge amounts of capital. In Europe as in America, credit unions or cooperative banks did not function as the financial arm of the other cooperative businesses. "One cannot think of a cooperative movement that is vigorous and expansive without its appeal to and application in the field of credit; a cooperativism lacking in this resource is senile, necessarily spineless, and has to remain confined to a field of craft activity and has to live in a small world, in circles that are domestic and modest." [17]

It must be remembered that Don José Maria, both during the Civil War and in the post-war period, had witnessed a great deal of dogmatic and ideological argument which prevented concrete achievements. In this context we can understand his impatience as he warns the social reformer to "beware of cooperatives who believe that enthusiasm can replace adequate capitalization, technology and planning." [18]

Most of his criticism of the traditional cooperative movement in Spain was related to the fact that it was mainly concentrated in the consumer and credit field with little development in the field of industrial production. Leaders in the cooperative movement have for a long time admitted this as a real problem and it is especially in the industrial field that capitalization, technology and planning are essential. Most Spanish cooperatives did not develop any sensitivity to these needs precisely because of the lack of experience in industry.

The fact that the Mondragon group is centred in the industrial sector sets it off as being quite different from the other parts of the European cooperative movement. In an article in *TU Lankide,* June 1980, Jesus Ginto points out an additional difference in terms of political affiliation. In Eastern Europe, the cooperatives were political in that they were part of a centralized state-planning system. Especially in the East and to some extent in the West, cooperative industries have been founded with a great deal of government support and as a result they have not developed their own autonomous base of support. In Western Europe, the cooperative movement has largely become politicized in the sense that cooperative organizations become linked to specific political parties. By contrast, the Mondragon cooperatives have considered it essential to remain politically neutral to maintain the unity of their work force as well as to develop wide community support.

However, it is too early to be definitive about whether Don José Maria was right or not in his assessment of the weakness of traditional cooperatives. In the mid-1990s, some traditional cooperative organizations still exist in Spain but they are struggling desperately to survive in the open competition of the Common Market. Side by side with these old cooperatives are newer hybrid forms of cooperative both in Mondragon and Valencia. Also, there are other new and hybrid forms of democratic ownership of the means of production. The newer cooperative forms such as Mondragon seem to be better-placed to survive in the new international order.

C: SOVIET MODEL

It is interesting that Don José Maria does not refer to a Marxist or a communist model. He points out that Marx did not consider the reality of the entity we call a business corporation. Corporate business complexes only became a world force during the twentieth century. Marx certainly talks about the processes of production and the factors involved, but Don José Maria claims that Marx did not foresee the importance and character of modern technology and did not understand how technology could reinforce and enhance the corporate entity as a self-generating and autonomous agent in society. Don José Maria is quite specific in treating the corporation as a distinct entity, going so far as to call the business corporation the unit or building block of society, in the way that some people would call the family the unit of society.

Don José Maria is quite careful not to blame Karl Marx for the faults of the Soviet economic system. Much of what he says in criticism of the capitalist model he also applies to the Soviet model. In both models, the power resides in the owner, regardless of whether the owner is a private person or a state. Although the context has changed so that the power of managers is limited by Soviet society, nevertheless the mental attitude of those who control is the same as that of capitalist managers. [19]

In the Soviet system, industrial corporations were given operational independence after 1923. Each corporation was controlled by three committees: 1) an administrative committee to look after the technical operation, 2) a labour committee to be responsible for the interests of the workers, and 3) the political committee or the party cell to look after political education. After 1927 it became necessary to impose central planning through five-year plans. However, the three committees made efficiency impossible. Finally, Stalin began to choose and train a new class of managers.

By 1970, Soviet managers were no longer from the ranks of the workers but were modern technocrats. It was only in 1958 that the worker committees were restored with rights to information, but not with control over management. In this respect the modern Soviet corporation resembles the modern American corporation. In both corporate systems the individual person is at the service of the economy, and thus becomes an object or tool in the system. It is true that American corporations were not controlled by a political party while the Soviet ones were controlled by the Communist party. However, the freedom from political control in America certainly did not translate into more freedom for workers to develop.

The tentative demise of the Soviet model, first under the cooperatization encouraged by Gorbachev in the late 1980s and then the struggling privatization of the Yeltsin period after 1991, has pointed out the terrible costs involved in moving from one system to another in a non-evolutionary way. If Don José Maria was around today he would have encouraged a gradual approach that built important intermediate models between capitalism and communism like the one he himself developed at Mondragon.

D: TOWARDS A NEW MODEL

Don José Maria's criticism of the conventional forms of the business corporation must be understood in the context of his overall intention of reform. Having concluded after many years of reflection and practical involvement that the business corporation is the basic cell or building block of a modern society, he saw that this is where reform must begin. Reform of the business corporation would necessarily involve reform of the person and reform of the total social system. "The necessity of this structural reform comes from two complementary sources," according to Don José Maria. "On one side from the corporation itself; and on the other from the workers whose dignity requires a corporate model distinct from the actual one whether it is capitalist or socialist."[20]

Since he found flaws in the capitalist, the Soviet and the traditional cooperative forms of business corporation, Don José Maria remained faithful to his method of searching and examining various experiences in economic development. He never really settled on any particular structure as being *the* answer nor developed a clear position on the theory of the corporation. His thinking on the reform of unsatisfactory models of business corporations developed on parallel lines with his understanding of cooperative corporations.[21]

Notes

1. *DJM*, vol 111, p. 67.
2. Milton Friedman, *Capitalism and Freedom*, Chicago: University of Chicago Press, 1962, p. 133. Emphasis added.
3. See Azurmendi, pp.411-412.
4. Don José Maria saw an inevitable decline in traditional corporations because of their approach to management and technology. See Azurmendi, p. 408.
5. It is noteworthy that the first publisher to translate the eight hundred page thesis on Mondragon theory by J. Azurmendi was Japanese.
6. *Cf.* Jack Quarter's book *The Canadian Social Economy,* Toronto: Lorimer, 1992. Algoma Steel will be discussed in Chapter 7 along with some other Canadian cases.
7. Berle and Means, *The Modern Corporation and Private Property*, 1931.
8. Edward Herman, *Corporate Control, Corporate Power,* New York: Cambridge University Press, 1981, p. 72.
9. L.C.B. Gower, *The Principles of Modern Company Law*, London: Stevens and Sons, 1969, p. 9.
10. Peter Drucker, *Post Capitalist Society*, New York: Harper Business, 1993.
11. *DJM*, FC-4-12.
12. Herbert Marcuse, *One Dimensional Man*, Boston: Beacon Press, 1964.
13. *DJM*, CLP-3-83.
14. *DJM*, FC-1-132.
15. See the Ten Principles in Chapter 2. The Mondragon Congress adopted these in *Introducion a la Experiecia Cooperativa de Mondragon*, Azatza, Otalora, Mondragon, 1997.

16. *DJM*, FC-1-140.
17. *DJM*, CLP-1-155.
18. *DJM*, FC-1-56.
19. *DJM*, CLP-3-91.
20. Azurmendi, p.421.
21. Azurmendi, p. 409.

CHAPTER 5

A NEW MODEL

In speaking of the new model proposed by Don José Maria, it is worth pointing out that there is nothing absolutely new concerning his ideas about business. In a talk given at a meeting of the Association of Cooperative Studies in Madrid in 1982, José Luis del Arco identifies the crucial factor as quite other than novelty. "His originality is founded on pragmatism. He did not accept pre-established and stereotyped formulas. He observed the social-economic reality avidly and applied whatever solution was most appropriate to the circumstances."[1]

What is interesting and useful is Don José Maria's practical synthesis which draws from a number of sources mentioned earlier. Each of the elements has been proposed before and each exists in practice somewhere. But the fact that we have had credit unions, or that we have had worker co-ops, and we have had research centres, and so on does not justify dismissing the Mondragon experiment. What is so important about Mondragon is that it is the only example of credit unions, producer co-ops and research centres and a university that operate as one integrated functional unit.

In his writings, Don José Maria oscillates between talking about the reform of the total society to achieve what he calls "the new order," and the reform of the "empresa." Fundamentally, what he proposes is a reform of the traditional corporation as the first step in the reform of the total society. This interpretation seems to fit when we see that he shifted from a notion of the family as the basic unit of society to the business corporation as the basic unit. There will be no change of society in general unless there is a change within the basic building blocks. The ideas proposed by Don José Maria, as well as the practical decisions he made, can only be understood in the context of his general goal of the total reform of society.

Don José Maria considers a cooperative business, like any concrete structure, only as a means or instrument on the road to this longer-term and more general goal of total reform, a goal which thus constitutes a criterion for day-to-day practical decisions. A particular action may not bring about the final solution, but if it points in the right direction it is good and acceptable. If it points in the opposite direction it is bad and not acceptable. He believed that there was a certain logic in history according to which the traditional forms of business would cave in as obsolete. He was optimistic that people would realize the need for a new form of business corporation that would be his idea for a new model, much more in keeping with a post-industrial society and adapted to human development. Thus his idea for a new model, what he calls cooperativism, is not a particular structure; it is rather a spirit which is permanent although the concrete structures are variable.

This chapter will consider the internal dynamics of the new corporate model, including the roles of management and workers as well as the relationship of the new corporation to the state and to society at large. On the subject of change it is noteworthy that an authority on Mondragon such as José Luis del Arco quotes Alex Laidlaw, a Canadian cooperative leader from Cape Breton Island, who calls for openness and change in the future. At a presentation to a conference of the International Cooperative Alliance in 1980 concerning the future of cooperatives, Dr. Laidlaw stated:

> It is said that institutions which oppose change will, in the end, be destroyed by it.... As a general rule, institutions are not changed from within, but through the force of external circumstances.... One thing is very clear; the cooperative movement of the future will be composed of a great variety of cooperatives, which will include some forms which do not now exist and which no one has yet imagined.[2]

The Mondragon cooperative corporation is one of those new forms being evolved.

A: THE COOPERATIVE CORPORATION

I shall use the term "cooperative corporation" to describe the new model discussed by Don José Maria. This terminology was in fact officially accepted at the annual Congress of Mondragon in1986. Don José Maria speaks of this model in contradistinction to the dominant capitalistic forms of business corporation which are mainly multinational. It is true that some of his criticisms apply to certain kinds of cooperatives. For example, in consumer cooperatives where the customer-members own the capital and the employees are subject to capital, the normal dynamic is the adversarial relationship of labour to capital. Sometimes the result is strikes of labour against management. Even so, it is best to think of the proposed model as a reaction to the dominant model of the stockholder business corporation where workers are merely hired labour. The difference is at the level of values rather than mechanical, structural details. As emphasized above, the basic difference concerns the goals and the spirit of the new model. Although this can never be completely spelled out, we can try to do so by picking out some of the distinctions which he raises in juridical, economic and human relations.

Juridical Relations . The conventional capitalist corporation is controlled by capital. Those who have the legal right to vote are those who own the capital, and their power of vote is in proportion to the amount of capital they possess. Thus, it is an association of capital. By contrast, the new model is an association of people, where one obtains the right to vote through being a member or associate and not through ownership of capital. In the Mondragon model the worker administers capital.[3] Although work-contracts are made under the new model, the traditional collective agreement does not make sense because it implies that the workers must bargain for a share of something that does not belong to them. In the new model, the negotiation concerns how much of the capital resources will be distributed to each of the associate workers and how much to the general society which is in indirect association. The result is a democratic group decision.

Economic Relations. Don José Maria insisted that a new structure and a new intention are not enough. They are necessary but not sufficient to constitute the new model. He speaks of an economic content and a dynamic centre of creativity and growth. He was tireless in his criticism of those who thought that good ideas, new intentions and new structures would suffice. He argued that besides being morally good, the new corporation must be a commercial powerhouse, able to have an economic impact on the community.

Central to the new model is the role of capital under the control of workers. Capitalism involves control by shareholders, impersonal faceless outsiders. In the Soviet model, with which Don José Maria also disagreed, the shift of control of capital to the state did not personalize production; rather it bureaucratized production. In the concrete, he opted for local control of capital. Thus, while capital growth is essential to all of his thinking, its role is modified significantly.

Juridically there are limitations to the ownership of capital by Mondragon workers. The only capital that a worker can actually withdraw at Mondragon is the amount in his or her capital account. The bulk of Caja financial assets is considered social capital which is administered and controlled by the workers collectively.

Although Don José Maria uses the term private ownership of capital, he does so in a special sense: The workers are basically stewards or administrators of capital. As good stewards, the workers have a social obligation to make sure that the capital grows. The growing capital is a necessary instrument in order to fulfil the social goal of helping the more needy parts of a society.

Human Relations. With modifications in the role of the factors of production, there follows a change in relationships on the human level. For instance, in the capitalist model, the intention and the goals are set by the owners of capital. Usually the intentions of the worker are different but the worker must submit. Also, the intention of the owner is often different from the intentions of the society at large. When capital is the source of relationships, conflict is inevitable.

Cooperative relations arise from a different source. The three dogmas of cooperativism that flow from the concept of "person" and "interpersonal relationships" are: 1) solidarity, 2) priority of the person over the instruments, and 3) the principle of distribution of results.[4]

Solidarity functions on two distinct levels. The first is internal, between workers within the cooperative corporation; the second is external, between the corporation and the rest of the society. "The linkage of work with social solidarity flows from the moment that the human subject perceives his or her limitations and weaknesses as an individual, and that solidarity humanizes and gives power to each of the worker members."[5] Obviously since "cooperativism is a complex of principles, a doctrine rather than a concrete structure," the successful implementation of the model will depend upon the human element, on how deeply the participants are committed to the principles of cooperativism. Because of this, the model must include education and development of the work force as well as effective means of communication between the associates.

The external level of solidarity in human relations is the relationship of one cooperative with other parts of society. Through participation in the cooperative corporation the worker is not only relating to other members of the corporation but is relating to the society at large, and is an actor in the process of total social change. Hard work and better productivity means more capital available to help others.

The new corporation is a "community" and communal relationships are taken in the sense of a common will. This unity of wills, rather than a juridical act, is what unites. Don José Maria sums it up as follows: "Let us consider that the enterprise ought to be a human community of activities and interests, based on private property and initiative [except in cases where the state intervenes for the common good] instituted to provide to the society a necessary service or useful production, for which it will receive an economic payment according to the services rendered, which is distributed to its members in a just manner."[6]

Other Aspects of the Coooperative Corporation

Don José Maria maintains the traditional factors of production, namely labour and capital, the latter with a transformed role, and then adds a third, "management." Especially in a technological society management itself becomes a key factor in economic production. Although distinct from the role of labour, the role of management also becomes transformed in the new model.

Concerning the question of whether a cooperative corporation can function in a capitalist society, he eventually affirmed that it could. Indeed, after analyzing events in the old Soviet system, he decided that the free market system was the best one available for the setting of prices. He concluded that if the new cooperative corporations could not adapt to the free market, then it was because of internal faults such as bad management, lack of capital, or an uneducated work force.

To sum up, Don José Maria would say that the economic function is the creative dynamic interaction of labour, management and capital which occurs in the context of a free market system. He never really discusses general questions of macroeconomics. He outlines the general goal of a new social order and then jumps to the level of microeconomic questions of organization.

B: A NEW ROLE FOR MANAGEMENT

Although the foundation of Don José Maria's model is deeply personalistic, the operational function—the provision of goods and services for a price—is clearly economic. As José Azurmendi points out, "this assumes that at the centre of the enterprise is a creative energy which is capable of conceiving the task, organizing the means necessary, etc. The process becomes more and more complex as society develops. 'Efficiency' becomes synonymous with 'viability.'"[7] Don José Maria's recognition of the organizational demands of business in the post-industrial society prompted him to regard management as a factor just as important as capital or labour. That he distinguishes sharply between labour and management flies in the face of traditional socialist theory, but he recognized it as a fact and even a necessary development.

What the manager encounters in cooperativism are three features which distiguish it from capitalism. These distinguishing features of cooperativism are:

1. The principle of personalism which implies commitment, open membership and mutual confidence.
2. The cooperative's not-for-profit character which is compatible with the legitimate return to the members for providing service to society.
3. The social character of the enterprise manifested in the existence of special funds allocated to the general society, sharing of surpluses among workers, participation of workers in control, and in the formation and education of all the membership.

Beyond these distinguishing features which largely are manifestations of the intention of the members and their long-term goals, the problems encountered by the manager of a cooperative corporation are very similar to those of a capitalistic corporation: for example, organization of capital, changing technology, communication, and forecasting of markets. [8]

In the new cooperative structure there are two levels of managerial function: a) The entrepreneurial function which implies the capacity to foresee and create; b) The directive function which involves the discipline of organization so as to implement a program of production resulting in the greatest possible return.

Don José Maria seems to regard entrepreneurial talent as being usually innate and a question of personality. He considers it a gift that some people have in the same sense that some people have the gift of music. Because of this, it is important to assess employees and promote those who do have this gift. Although he says that every worker should be an entrepreneur, continually looking for ways to improve production, the necessity to identify those especially gifted is a requirement of good management.

Besides the capacity for risk and the will to reinvest, the entrepreneurial spirit required of the good manager involves the freedom and capacity to make decisions. Not everybody has this capacity, so the group chooses the best person and they channel decision-making to the one who can best act on their behalf. At times management will also have to admit its limitations and solicit outside help. [9]

Just as the entrepreneurial function of management is not taken in an exclusive sense, but rather is a key function of management which is also encouraged among employees, so also the organizing function is not exclusive. The good manager is one who coordinates the activities of others about him and encourages them to take responsibility.

Although workers have a strong say in the social role of the enterprise, and in the general plan of operation, it is quite clear that they do not have a great deal of say in the day to day financial and economic operation of the enterprise. Authority is granted to the Board of Directors by the General Assembly of workers. The board, in turn, delegates authority to the general manager. The general manager in collaboration with his or her management team is clearly in control with an organizational structure which is quite hierarchical. As Bradley and Gelb point out, "Formally the organizational structure of a typical Mondragon cooperative does not differ too greatly from that of a capitalist corporation."[10]

Don José Maria regarded management as the most sensitive point in the enterprise. Once the yearly program has been approved by the social structures, it will be administered by senior management. Regarding "the application of the norms and development of the program, it must be precisely recognized that in its configuration the technical aspect must take precedence, and its fundamental structural line will be vertical and after having applied on the social side a democratic projection, it will work out to be rigid and demanding. Management is judged by results, but on the balance sheet, the social and human needs will be considered as well as the economic."[11]

He goes on to say that "The highest post in this pyramid, which forms the enterprise, is the one occupied by management. Using the simile of political life, it can be said that the manager is in the enterprise what the prime minister is to the legislature. The human community represented by the board of directors fixes objectives, a policy to follow and delegates to the manager the implementation or execution of these....It remains very clear that the final decision, the sovereignty of the cooperative, is in the hands of the members, in the general assembly, through its legitimate representatives, the board of directors."[12]

According to Don José Maria's thinking, the cooperative corporation would have all the means available to capitalistic corporations plus the added moral force of cooperative principles. With this advantage, it would not only compete, but do better than conventional business. However, this puts a greater demand upon management. Not only must the manager have all the skills of a conventional manager, but also the extra ones of personal commitment and the ability to share and communicate with the total work force. In order to maintain the common intention essential to the cooperative approach, a flow of information in both directions is essential.

Don José Maria considered much of the democratization of decision-making in traditional corporations, whether cooperative or private, to be spurious in that the manager would take over when he didn't like the decision. Rather, he favoured decentralization as long as the definition of functions and responsibilities were clearly spelled out.

He mentions such rules for management as:
1. Absolute independence for the manager in the exercise of his duties;
2. Delegation of functions to other personnel;
3. A good and clear personnel policy;
4. Attention to questions of human relationships.

In discussing the notion of a manager, Don José Maria emphasizes continuing self development. He points out that managers have a social and moral responsibility to continue their education and to keep up to date on the latest business techniques. Also there is a great need of personal honesty. As the enterprise develops, it can happen that the operation grows beyond the capacity of the manager. An honest manager will admit this and gracefully step down to let someone else take over.

The fact that Mondragon managers receive only 58 per cent of the average wage of equivalent managers in capitalist enterprises shows that the principle of personal commitment is taken very seriously. Recognizing the difficulty of maintaining a spirit of altruism and social commitment among managers, Don José Maria considered management development an essential part of his model. It was expected and is the case that the majority of managers do come from within the ranks of the work force.

C: ROLE OF WORKERS

The term "worker" can be understood at two levels. There is the level at which one is employed in and working for the enterprise. Then there is the more general level of being a member of society at large and working for society. The main goal of the worker is to build a new society which is more just and democratic than the current one. It involves breaking down divisions between groups in society where one group is more privileged at the expense of the majority of the others. It is important to remember this more general intention because it explains why the basic concern is never simply the legalistic or mechanical function of a worker in one particular model of business. The concern is about how the total life of the worker will be affected. The democratic experience of work is meant to spill over into the rest of one's life.

Don José Maria says "Fundamental cooperativism is an organic process of experiences, characterized precisely by adherence to moral values, by the prevalence of man as such over the other factors more or less instrumental in every economic process and activity."[13]

The primary level is the worker in the service of the particular enterprise, and the enterprise rewards him or her for this. The general level is the worker and the whole enterprise in the service of the general society, and society rewards the enterprise as such for this. For workers the enterprise is the basis of their economic lives. The immediate goal, though not the principal one, is to provide a living for the employees.

There is one major point at which the worker can affect the actual government of the enterprise, and this is through the General Assembly where the workers elect the Board of Directors. However, this is the key control mechanism and through it workers can dismiss their management. This is in contrast to some French models where great emphasis is placed on worker committees participating in day to day management. In the model proposed by Don José Maria, the management function is distinct from that of the worker function. The lines of authority are hierarchical and responsibility is clearly pinpointed. Nevertheless, worker development is supposed to be promoted in diverse ways, such as skill improvement, rotation of jobs, continuing education, and experimentation in the work process with, for example, quality circles.

Don José Maria's option for hierarchical management appears to be a result of his analysis of industrial evolution. He considered that the nature of a high-tech industry is such that many years of complex preparation is required to produce a good business manager. Business decisions are such that they are not enhanced by group participation on a general level. They are most efficiently made when left to managers and management teams. Don José Maria believed that in a sound educational program for workers, managers would naturally evolve from within. Efforts should be made to find such individuals with entrepreneurial talent and to promote them for the common good.

Don José Maria also demanded concrete participation by the workers. In his model each worker is required to contribute capital. The worker, in practice as well as in theory, is required to be as self-sufficient as possible. Participation in the government of the enterprise goes along with participation in the gathering and creation of the capital required to make the enterprise productive, and a creator of new wealth.

Since the worker is now a proprietor and administrator there is no longer the old fear of redundancy, of being cast aside in the face of new technology. Now the worker welcomes new technology as belonging to him or her and making work and the enterprise more productive and useful to society. As long as the enterprise exists, the worker has a secure job. There may be salary reductions decided by the general assembly, but still the worker has the right to participate in a job as long as the group rules are followed. Because of the necessity of closing out some enterprises with time, the larger Mondragon family of cooperative corporations arranges mobility of workers among its different enterprises. Although nobody can guarantee jobs absolutely, there is a very effective moral guarantee.

In theory as well as in demonstrated practice, less supervision is required in this model because workers are caring for their own property and that of their neighbours, not somebody else's. In the traditional business there is a divided intention. The owners and management have one intention and the workers have another. Here there is a unity of intention which should lead to a unity of action. In order for this to be true in practice and not just in theory, great attention must be paid to communications within the enterprise, in both directions.

In their systematic analysis of Mondragon attitudes, Bradley and Gelb conclude that, although the structure is hierarchical, there is a very high trust level and a unity of wills.[14] The workers know about and agree with management strategies. It is my conclusion that the hierarchical structure is not for the purpose of imposing an intention that is alien to the intention of the worker, or a benefit that is opposed to the benefit of the worker, but rather to expedite decision-making and identify responsibility. Thus the hierarchical system allows the goals of the workforce to be achieved.

Don José Maria promoted the technical formation of workers and the introduction of world-class technology in order to survive in the competitive world. At the same time he never lost sight of the priority of the worker as a human person. Jesus Larranaga, one of the five founders of ULGOR, quotes him in his final years;

> There are some values that we have promoted too much: efficiency in work with no limits, viability, development, growth, but now is the time for us to put other values in their place and give primacy to friendship, conviviality, and communication. This is to see in the other person something that is above all material values.[15]

D: THE MONDRAGON COOPERATIVE CORPORATION

The Cooperative Corporation itself is a moral entity having responsibility at three levels: 1) towards the individual employees, 2) towards the cooperative corporations which make up the Mondragon family, and 3) towards the general society of which it is the basic unit. "As the family is the cell of the society, the enterprise is the cell of the world of production. All reform must begin here—reform of the person, reform of the enterprise, reform of the system."[16]

As a microcosm of the general society, the enterprise must practice all the virtues demanded of the total society such as respect for the members, personal development and educational programs, social security and distributive justice. Each cooperative corporation in the Mondragon complex shares a common philosophy spelled out in the Contract of Association. The principle of solidarity requires the members to share both in good times and in bad times. In order to make solidarity a concrete reality and not simply theoretical, enterprises are required to develop common work policies, to share capital, to share in purchases and in sales and so on. Permeating so much of the model is the old Platonic as well as the Biblical image of the human body: no matter how big or small the organ or member, the health of each is essential for the health of the total body so that the capacity of the totality is greater that the capacity of the sum of the parts.

The different cooperatives within the Mondragon complex make up a living body. Each part has its own identity but yet can only function as part of a larger whole. There is a whole variety of criss-crossing connections between the Technical College, the factories, the research centres, the Caja (cooperative bank) and the social security system; each part depends upon the other. The model is a biological one as opposed to a mechanical one.

Unequivocally, Don José Maria states that each individual cooperative corporation as well as the Mondragon complex as a whole is accountable to the total society. Like Kropotkin, a well-known Russian social critic, he warns that cooperatives are very susceptible to collective egoism. Some cooperators have the mistaken notion that if they look after the interests of their members, then they have looked after the interests of the society. It would be very easy for the very successful Fagor Electronic companies to vote themselves higher wages and forget about the rest of the unemployed workers in their country. For Don José Maria this would be capitalism under the cooperative name. For him what is wrong with capitalism is not capital, but rather the egoistical motives of the owners of capital.

He wrote: "Cooperatives have a community dimension which obliges them not only to give satisfaction to their own membership, but also to fulfil a social function through its structures. First, we must consider that the enterprise is not only our property, and therefore we only have the use of it, and we must give an account of how we use it...calculations cannot be thought of exclusively pleasing the membership, but rather of serving to fulfil more perfectly the mission that society has confided to us."[17]

While admitting that certain kinds of goods are so essential to the common good that they must be publicly owned, Don José Maria proposed that basic economic production must be left in private hands. Obviously in a highly technological age most of the production will be done by corporations, with marginal activities left to small business. Thus Don José Maria implies that the new model of enterprise will depend upon the free will of its members to do what is best for society. The new model offers a means for personal and individual creativity to benefit all.

As Don José Maria put it, "The industrial corporation, whose primordial function is the creation or transformation of goods required to satisfy human needs, is an institution of such vital service for our society that the private property involved must remain subordinated to the common good in greater measure than other types of private property."[18] So, although the corporation must be able to act independently of the state, this does not mean that it has arbitrary freedom. It means rather that the submission to social needs must rely on a moral force and not a legal one. The need for continual investigation, discussion and education concerning the state of society and what is best to be done underlies the moral imperative.

Though the social responsibility is highlighted, Don José Maria warns that the business of the corporation is economic and not political. He saw the danger that the corporation could become totalitarian, and try to control all aspects of life. Thus he insisted that the corporation be politically neutral. This is in contradistinction to the Italian model of a worker cooperative which chooses political alliances. The Mondragon worker, through participation in the corporation, looks after fundamental economic needs. All workers in an enterprise should be united in this common task even though they have different political opinions. As noted above, Don José Maria encouraged workers to be politically involved as individuals, but not as members of the corporation.

The free market, in Don José Maria's thinking, is a device for society to decide whether it values the service being proposed by the corporation. "In our conception of the enterprise," he wrote, "we conceive profit as the payment for the utility that has been rendered to society. It must be admitted however that the profit subsists if the service rendered is morally indifferent. But when the opposite is evident and the useful is replaced by what is harmful and dishonest, then the profit is not justified, nor in reality is the permanence of the enterprise."[19] He believed that the basic idea of the enterprise is service, so the sale price cannot be merely a question of commercial circumstance but it must take into account the common good. This was the aspect of the cooperative business tradition that attracted him most. As he understood it, "Cooperatives, in so far as they are business enterprises, assume the responsibility of creating jobs and promoting development."[20]

In general the objectives of Don José Maria's new model enterprise are twofold: first, "to humanize the economy and to improve people. This involves a faith in the ability of the worker." And second, "Social promotion so that there are values superior to profit." Then he reiterates his overall aim. "The objective is the economic, political, social and cultural improvement of the workers and society in general."[21] He even restates this concept in stronger language: "Our goal is more than simple options for individual improvement. It is more. If the cooperative enterprise does not serve for more, the world of work has the right to spit in our faces."[22]

E: EVALUATION AND REPLICABILITY

Clearly, Don José Maria's new model is different. Some of the contrasts are as follows:

CAPITALIST	SOVIET	MONDRAGON
Primacy of Capital	Primacy of Bureaucracy	Primacy of Community
Subordination of Labour	Subordination of Labour	Subordination of Capital
Abuse of Community	Irrelevance of Community	Primacy of Community

The question is often asked: Can this alternative corporate model be applicable and useful in other communities and nations? To answer the question, I first examine the three basic elements in Don José Maria's conception of the new corporate model. I then go on to evaluate the validity of the standard objections to the transfer of these elements to a new context.

In his conception of this renewed corporation, Don José Maria speaks of three basic elements:

I.   the intention or motivating force which directs the actions of the corporation;
II. the technological capacity or the machinery that makes it possible to achieve economic goals;
III. the role of the individual within the corporation.

Motivating Intentions. For Don José Maria, the corporation is like a human person and should have social motivations and good intentions. He stated: "Let us consider that the enterprise ought to be a human community of activities and interests based on private property and initiative (except in cases where the state intervenes for the common good), instituted to provide the society with services and products, for which it will receive an economic recompense according to the services rendered, which is distributed among its members in a just manner."[23]   Since it is a human community, this means that it can have motivations beyond profit maximization as the determinant of action. For some extremists this opinion is not practical but, if we look at more modern thinking, we find that very serious analysts now agree on the importance of a corporation having a clear moral purpose. In the *Harvard Business Review*, Kenneth Goodpaster writes: "We think an analogly holds between the individual and the corporation. If we analyze the concept of moral responsibility as it applies to persons we find that projecting it to corporations as agents in society is possible."[24]

Technological Capacity. One of the most striking aspects of the model is the great emphasis on technique and technology. The theory as well as the practice is infused with an almost fierce attachment to the necessity of being on the cutting edge of the most advanced technology available.

Some say that this is the result of Don José Maria's impressions of the Spanish Civil War. He noted the great idealism on the side of the Republican forces and especially the International Brigades who came from all over the world to fight in their noble cause. However, many of the regiments were characterized also by great ideological debates. At times the divisions at the level of theory made it almost impossible for troops on the same side to work together. Amidst all of this Don José Maria saw Hitler's Air Force come in to help Franco by bombing the Basques' most ancient and sacred city of Guernica. The idealism of the Republican forces was no match for the precision and efficiency of Hitler's technology. Some people of high ideals have maintained that they would rather die and see all their troops defeated than to compromise on an ideal.

Don José Maria considered this to be nonsense and even immoral from a Christian point of view. It is moral to die for people, but it is fanaticism to die for ideals. You do something and then you reflect on what you did to make sure that it is consistent with your principles and what you want to achieve. If you really want to achieve something of economic significance, you must use good technology.

An Association of Persons. The third important element to be evaluated is the role of individual persons in this new model. The worker or member is first of all a person. A cooperative corporation is an association of persons rather than an association of capital.

This means that the person gets the vote, rather than the capital getting the vote in proportion to quantity. In other words the problem of capitalism is that votes are assigned because of the amount of money that one has as opposed to being assigned on the basis of being a human person with intrinsic value. As the personalists said, it is more important "to be" than "to have." The role of the worker is thus very different in the Mondragon model because in the final analysis the individual worker is both owner and controller of the corporation. This is clearly different from the usual model of workers and managers being adversaries on opposite sides of the table.

A Repeatable Combination

Among the above three elements, the role of technology in Mondragon is not very different from its role in the regular corporate world. However, the combination of superior technology with a corporate community motivation along with a personalistic role for workers is unusual and different. The big question is always, "Can the Mondragon model be replicated?" Bradley and Gelb seem to be quite pessimistic about the possibility of this kind of experiment working in other places. However, strange as it may seem, when I analyze their findings, my conclusions are quite different from theirs.

In their surveys, Bradley and Gelb discovered that a key factor within Mondragon was the personal attachment of the managers, as well as the general workforce, to their community. A test in the probation period of a new worker is his or her ability to fit and belong to the community of workers as a social group. The fact that they come from the same villages, go to the same bars, belong to the same clubs, has a cohesive effect and develops solidarity that carries over into the economic sphere. Without this sort of social and personal commitment, the experiment is difficult to replicate. Bradley and Gelb conclude that these values cannot be relied upon as part of the economic equation.

I disagree with this conclusion. Underneath their discussion there appears to be the old dogma still held by some economists that "values" and "facts" are distinct and that economics is about "facts" and not "values." The objection by such economists that we cannot have an efficient economic enterprise when values and social commitment come into play may not be founded on scientific considerations at all. It may simply be an assumption based on what is, regrettably, common practice. It is a fact that most of the industrialized world promotes worker mobility. Many governments encourage workers to follow the geographically shifting demands of the market. It is typical in large industrial centres that people do not know each other's background or much about their social life. Entertainment is quite anonymous. That is the reality of our large cities. However, simply because the reality is that way does not logically lead to the conclusion that it *must* be that way.

There is no well founded scientific argument that the dynamic of economics has to be impersonal and divorced from all social and traditional dynamics. The mechanical view of economics seems to work well when we are doing macroeconomic models. Part of this economic understanding involves the free and easy mobility of workers to serve the needs of the changing techno-industrial system. The underlying and justifying claim here is always that this is the way that wealth is created. Further, it is claimed that this is part of a "scientific law" which is part of the foundation of "rational" economics. This dogma has yet to be proved.

A fascinating angle to be considered is that the worst pockets of unemployment and depression in the industrialized world are in the marginal and outlying regions. These are usually regions where people are more socially cohesive, where they are less inclined to leave their family and friends for economic advancement. Perhaps, the Mondragon model is not well suited to an urban impersonal environment; but it may be very well suited to the regions of industrialized countries which have stable social structures along with depressed economies.

In their unhopeful conclusions, Bradley and Gelb point out that they are assuming the usual economic parameters: "Underlying our discussion is the same self-centred individualistic human model common to conventional economic theory."[25] However, I do not accept this presupposition and neither did Don José Maria. In many cases human nature is egoistical, but contrary to what as so many conventional economists assume, it doesn't have to be that way. The whole thrust of the personalist tradition discussed in Chapter Three points in the opposite direction. We might do very well to apply this kind of economic development strategy, which is based upon human solidarity, in those regions which are most deprived. Perhaps in the long run, what is a disadvantage (lack of self-centeredness) will turn into an advantage.

It should be clear by now that the neo-classical view of economics is largely a question of faith and dogma and not of necessity. Since other views are quite possible there is complete justification in proposing personalistic and social motivation as a tremendous creator of wealth. Also, it is not irrational to prefer the organic and living paradigm of economics to the mechanical one. The debate between these two kinds of economic views cannot be resolved in any absolute way. It does seem to be largely a matter of faith and even of ideology for many. In view of many negative experiences with religious and ideologically bound economic systems as a method of decision, the empirical approach of deciding on the merits of proven cases seems to be the most prudent way. We will then have a method that is value-based and a matter of faith, but it will not be faith alone. It will be values tested in action. Since values play a key role, they can be articulated and discussed as practical elements in the context of successful cases.

Many observers of the Mondragon enterprises remark that these internationally competitive companies look very much like any modern capitalist corporation. On the surface this may be so, especially if one takes only a small slice of time or only one or two aspects. However, when we observe the operations over a long term and analyze the life of the worker within the enterprise, the differences become apparent. In a recent official publication, the contrast was laid out in the following manner:

COOPERATIVE MODEL	CAPITALISTIC MODEL
1. Priority of persons, professionalism, excellence of products, satisfaction of clients. Viability is not a primary objective; rather it is a consequence.	1. Priority of the financial, meaning the highest and most rapid return on investment.
2. Persons form part of the enterprise. They are part of the purpose and participate in management.	2. Persons are considered as means and are expendable.
3. The contract is with society and the commitment is to the development of the business. The tendency is to lifetime employment with cooperation between workers and capital.	3. The contract is with a worker and the commitment is to a task. The relation is one of confrontation between labor and capital.
4. Education is considered an investment in a human, social and technical sense. It is capitalization through professional competence.	4. Priority of technical training with no attention to other types of education.
5. Policies which tend to a long term and social good.	5. Policies which are short term and directed to short term profits.
6. Priority to growth through self development of the enterprise.	6. The enterprise is available for sale to highest bidder—which usually means down-sizing.
7. Difficulty in accessing external capital markets.	7. Ease of access to external capital markets.
8. Power is shared between the various departments; technical, commercial and finance.	8. Power lies mainly in the hands of the financiers.
9. The profits and losses are shared amongst all proportionately.	9. The profits are privatized and the losses are socialized.
10. Personnel policy is oriented to men and women as persons invested with dignity.	10. Personnel policy considers employees as entities with a capacity for work.

Source: "Introduccion a la Experiencia Cooperativa," Otalora, 1997.

While admitting that not all capitalistic corporations follow the hard-line policies outlined above, we must admit that most trans-national corporations, outside of Japan, do. This is especially evident in the mergers and downsizing that has been going on in recent years. When we contrast this with the Mondragon commitment to life-time employment and the excellent packages given to retirees, then we see that there are very deep and radical differences in the value systems and that they do make a difference.

By demanding an empirical element in discussions about what is the best kind of economic enterprise, we avoid much empty debate. Consistent with this position, it is important to search for actual cases where a community oriented approach achieved tangible and significant economic results. Those who hold the view that the mechanical egoistical type of system produces significant wealth do have a great deal of empirical argument in their favour at this time. Mondragon is an empirical argument on the other side.

However, one swallow does not make the spring. There are other cases, and the most interesting one is Valencia.

Notes

1. José Luis del Arco, *"El Complejo Cooperativo de Mandragon"* Meeting of the Association of Cooperative Studies, Madrid, 1982, p. 59.
2. Unpublished talk, St. Francis Xavier Department, 1980.
3. Azurmendi, p. 437.
4. Azurmendi, p. 471-72.
5. *DJM*, CLP, 111, 235.
6. Azurmendi, p. 416.
7. Azurmendi, p. 420.
8. Azurmendi, p. 490-96.
9. Azurmendi, p. 504.
10. Bradley and Gelb, "The Replicablility and Sustainability of the Mondragon Experiment," *British Journal of Industrial Relations*, vol. XX, No. 1 (March 1982), pp. 20-33.
11. *DJM*, CLP-111, p. 71-73.
12. *DJM*, FC-11, p. 239
13. *DJM*, FC-11 p. 189-190.
14. Bradley and Gelb, *op. cit.*
15. Jesus Larranaga, *Don José Maria y la Experiencia Cooperativa de Mondragon*, Mondragon: Caja Laboral, 1981, p. 226.
16. *DJM*, CLP -111, p.·82-83.
17. *DJM*, IB 261 or A2 515.
18. Azurmendi, p. 421.
19. Azurmendi, p. 422.
20. Azurmendi, p.508.

21. Azurmendi, p. 475
22. FC III—76
23. Azurmendi, p. 416.
24. "Can a Corporation have a Conscience?" *Harvard Business Review,* Jan.-Feb, 1982, p. 133.
25. Bradley and Gelb, *op. cit.* p. 217.

CHAPTER 6

THE VALENCIA EXPERIMENT

Although much smaller than Mondragon, the Valencia experiment is similar in many ways, mainly because the organizers regarded Mondragon as their model. Valencia itself is a city of over one half million, approximately 1,000 kilometers south of Mondragon. Situated in Northeast Spain, it borders the Mediterranean, south of Barcelona, and is part of the province of Catalonia.

As with the Basques, language was a justice issue in the Valencia region. Franco, with his centrist policies, made their traditional dialect, a variation of the Catalan language, illegal. Catalonians have an ancient Latin-based language that reflects both Spanish and French. Most Catalonians were in fierce opposition to Franco, and the people in the small villages continued to speak Catalan, their traditional language.[1]

A: BEGINNINGS AND DEVELOPMENT

The beginnings of the Valencia economic experiment go back to the 1960s when all of Europe was alive with young people questioning the established institutions. Feelings were particularly strong in Spain because the dictatorship of Franco was still in force. Under Franco there was a good deal of poverty and difficult working conditions existed for the ordinary people. Social injustice was evident at many levels.

One organization that was particularly strong around the small villages in the Valencia region was Rural Christian Action. Young activists in this movement were inspired by the renewed Church thinking that came with the Second Vatican Council in Rome. This council called upon lay Christians to take responsibility for making society more just and closer to the ideals of the early Church.

Caixa Valencia

Josep Soriano. Josep Soriano was one of these young activists. When Soriano went to university, he continued discussions with other young people about social justice, and held on to his vision of a renewed society that would be kinder and more just. Ironically, this vision conflicted with that of the older generation. As is often the case with young people from working class families, their parents wanted their children to "get ahead." They did not want them to become farmers. Nevertheless, Josep and his friends wanted to go back and help their own people. Josep himself did begin the study of law but he did not want to become a lawyer; he wanted a more active involvement. He dropped his law studies and took up journalism.

Young Activist Group. These young people were serious about their Christian values, their opposition to the Franco establishment and their positive commitment to transform society. Within this particular circle, there was an older student who had worked in the construction industry where he had come in contact with cooperative housing. Eventually his contribution to the discussion led to the idea of the group going back to their region and developing a housing program. The group also included a young architect who had studied in Barcelona as well as a young man who had studied business administration. With this kind of expertise among them, the members felt ready to launch a project.

In 1969, after intensive discussion about the condition of Catalonia and especially their own villages which bordered Valencia, they established a housing cooperative, Covipar, as a concrete activity through which they could translate their convictions into action. Eventually Covipar generated their consulting company, their cooperative bank and their factories.

In those early years, Josep Soriano worked as a journalist during the day and on the housing cooperative at night. Most of the time other members of the group divided their time similarly between a day job and night time attention to the co-op. For periods of time, some of them had only part-time wages. A number of their wives worked and were able to provide income.

Contact with Don José Maria. In 1971 the group heard about the Mondragon experiment and made a trip to visit Don José Maria and his associates. Don José Maria was quite blunt with them. He told them that it was fine to provide housing if that was all they wanted to do. However, he pointed out that their system would never allow them to build an equity and a capital base permitting them to go on and do other things. His suggestion was that they should form another company which could sell its services to the housing cooperative, thus creating income and equity.

Don José Maria made a clear distinction between a group wishing to supply services, whether in the form of housing or in the form of grocery distribution, and a group building an economic instrument which could create wealth and jobs for its community. To become an economic instrument means developing a capital base and building up equity. In the Mondragon approach there is always expansion with one enterprise being the trigger to get another enterprise going. On their return to Valencia, the Covipar group set up a new consulting collective called Coinser.

The peak of activity of the housing project was around 1978. By then, they had organized and assisted 120 cooperative housing groups which resulted in three thousand living units. During 1978-79 they were working with sixty projects which included a grocery chain and a credit union. But in 1980 the demand for housing cooperatives dropped off. By 1983 only ten members were working in Coinser and they were building only single family units.

As Don José Maria had predicted, this type of activity did not have a long term growth potential. Once individuals obtained a home and secured a personal mortgage then there was no more commercial involvement with the Covipar. They had received an important service but the cooperative had not set up a method of structured involvement to encourage further job creation and wealth creation.

Fortunately, Soriano and his team had been working with a variety of groups on a variety of fronts. By 1975 they recruited a lawyer and also attempted to expand their technical capacity. After the discussions with Don José Maria, they began to see themselves as a team of people working through whatever juridical structure was convenient. The name or the form of the company might change, but they remained the same in their commitment to a better and more just society through economic activity.

In the mid 1970s the group reviewed their personal involvement and made an important decision which affected later developments. They could have limited membership in the group to themselves and eventually they would have become wealthy. Instead, they welcomed new member workers. They regarded the equity they were building to be not only in the form of money, but also in the form of a human resource team which, like an organic structure, would need to grow.

Through their housing work the Coinser group had a cash flow and used it over the years to subsidize their activity in other areas. As a strategy the group decided to concentrate on those areas which were less developed in the economy of the Valencia region. Their dedication to continual expansion was possible only through a certain amount of sacrifice. The leaders were able to keep their own wages low because their wives worked and they themselves lived modestly. They made these sacrifices, not because they were saints, but to make the business work. Today, their wages are as good and usually better than in comparable businesses.

Addressing Educational Needs. Another need in the Valencia area was educational. Schools, at that time, provided education for those who wanted to become professionals such as lawyers, doctors, and clergy. There were no structures to prepare young people who wanted to become farmers. Thus between 1975 and 1978 the group spent a great deal of time setting up agricultural schools. In 1976 they also established a non-agricultural school which became a polytechnical college called Florida. During this period they were so busy with the schools that there was no time to set up other businesses. At that point they decided to let these schools run on their own so that they could devote their time to the development of other types of business.

Failures and Success. Over these years the team made regular trips to Mondragon to observe developments there and tried to imitate them at home. Examples of failure in these attempts indicate that they had not adopted crucial aspects of the Mondragon model. In one instance they wanted to duplicate the attempt to promote female entrepreneurship which Mondragon had developed in a cooperative exclusively for women. Coinser also organized a female cooperative called Covamur. There was great deal of good will but they could not recruit the required professional management, so it failed. They also organized a construction cooperative, intending to steer some of their contracts to this company. This did not work very well as most of the tradesmen preferred to receive a secure salary from a conventional company and did not want to get involved in a cooperative. A newly-organized furniture cooperative and a textile cooperative, where there was a great deal of enthusiastic ideology but little technical competence, did not work well either.

During the 1970s the first major project that succeeded in recruiting competent professionals and technical staff-members was Consum, the grocery chain. As this initiative grew it became evident that a financial instrument was needed. Thus, in 1978, they followed the example of Mondragon and set up a community bank or credit union called the Caixa.

Research and Development. As in the case of Mondragon, research and development was at first done by the Caixa. However, the task of being a developer, advisor, troubleshooter and lender of money became too complex for the Valencia Caixa. In 1983 the Caixa decided to hive off the technical consulting function as a separate business entity. Those who worked for the Entrepreneurial Division of the Caixa now became employees or members of a new workers' cooperative called Grupo Audit.

Of the forty employees in Grupo Audit in 1990, only twenty were voting members. The others were aspiring members. This is the usual pattern. Those who want to belong to a workers' co-op in this tradition usually have to spend at least a year in a probationary stage.

Luis Ferre. During the 1960s Luis Ferre was an activist in the local labour movement. He was one of a large number of his co-workers in a glass factory who wanted something better for themselves. Especially during the early seventies, their future looked precarious. This was the time of the oil crisis and the resulting economic dislocation. His group knew about the traditional cooperatives and so they decided to break away on their own and form a cooperative to run their own business. But first there were political difficulties to surmount. Meetings of more than four people were forbidden at that time unless the government of Franco gave special permission. Fortunately, Ferre and his friends were on good terms with a sympathetic local pastor. This pastor encouraged them and allowed them to use Church buildings in secret for their meetings.

Ferre also knew Josep Soriano and they shared the same vision. Ferre approached the Caixa group for help. Although the Caixa group could not provide much capital, they were able to advise on the basic structures which they had learned about in Mondragon. This was the beginning of what turned out to be La Mediterranea, a successful new enterprise within the Valencia experiment.

B: THE PARTS (TO 1988)

COVIPAR (Cooperativa de Viviendas Populares): In 1969, the group began their housing cooperative by forming Covipar. In nine years the housing cooperative grew to three thousand units. It based its organization on group purchase of land and a group mortgage with members achieving ownership of their own houses when the mortgage was paid off. In effect Josep Soriano and his group acted as developers and provided people with affordable housing. They contracted out the actual architectural work and construction.

COINSER (Cooperativa Industrial de Servicios): In 1971 the Covipar group set up Coinser, a kind of consulting company which sold its services to the housing cooperative. It worked well, especially since the members of the group were still subsidizing the company through much donated time. In Coinser the number of employees ranged from five to eighteen, depending upon the amount of work. Their method was simple. They charged a flat fee of four to five per cent of the gross cost of the project. Their fee did not cover architectural costs. In 1975 they earned $40,000. Instead of distributing all of it to themselves as wages, they took out only $20,000 and kept the other $20,000 as seed capital for other enterprises.

Actually in these initial years, Soriano and his team, all of them committed volunteers, constituted the core staff of all their operations. Eventually their consulting function passed to the entrepreneurial division of the Caixa and finally to Grupo Audit.

CONSUM: Up until 1970 the only cooperatives in the Valencia region were agricultural. Hence Soriano and his group chose to work on the establishment of cooperative consumer stores in 1976. This was the forerunner of the Consum chain of cooperative stores which sold mainly groceries. This retail system was modeled upon the Mondragon chain of Eroski stores. In 1992 the Consum chain in Valencia established a working relationship with the Eroski chain in Mondragon.

CAIXA POPULAR: When the Coinser group began to plan for Consum they realized that a financial institution would be required. In 1977 they applied for and got authorization to operate a credit union. The new Caixa Popular began operations in 1978 with the staff of the old Entrepreneurial and Community Division transferring to it. By 1980 the Caixa was able to pay this staff their full salaries. Effectively, the Caixa (credit union) now became the mother of new enterprise development.

The Caixa is a second level cooperative. The voting members are cooperatives and staff. When it began in 1978 there were eight member cooperatives including Coinser. By 1980 there were close to twenty cooperative members. In 1983 there were thirty and in 1990 there were eighty.

Over the years there developed a set of rules amongst the members of this new cooperative complex. The Caixa promised to lend the members required capital, while the member cooperatives promised to use the services of its entrepreneurial division. It was a two-way street. Underlying all these interactions was a clear commitment to recruit highly competent staff and to develop the existing staff to the highest possible professional level. The unifying force was the Caixa.

Although the Caixa is dedicated to the establishment of new enterprises, most of the capital comes from non-cooperative sources. Eighty per cent of the deposits are from private individuals but 70 per cent of the investment is with cooperative enterprises.

GRUPO AUDIT: The services offered by Grupo Audit are legal, fiscal, accounting and general management services. They do consulting on strategic planning, market analysis, and engineering studies as well as various computer-based services. They consider the social economy to be their specialty. Although their target market is Valencia, they also have an office in Madrid. As with the Caixa their clientele now goes beyond cooperatives who, in fact, formed only 50 per cent of the client base in 1990. The other 50 per cent are public and private institutions as well as private businesses. Staff includes lawyers, psychologists, engineers and business administration graduates. Profits average around five to ten per cent. Monolo, the manager, likes to point out that, while the growth rate of consulting companies in Spain during 1989 was 30 per cent, Grupo's growth rate was approximately 50 per cent.

The group has specialized in client companies who are part of the social economy, especially in the start-up and the expansion phases. However, Grupo Co-op is evolving and increasing. The number of non-cooperative clients has increased from zero in 1983 to 50 per cent in 1990. Monolo claims that the problems encountered by traditional family firms are very similar to the kinds of problems encountered in cooperative enterprises. In both kinds of businesses, personal interaction plays a special role. Thus Grupo Audit is especially suited to dealing with their needs.

The success of the Grupo is reflected in its rapid growth. In 1983, there were eight people involved in the transfer from the Caixa's Entrepreneurial Division to Grupo Audit. Sales were twelve million pesetas. By 1989, a brief six years later, there were thirty employees with sales of 125 million pesetas. In 1990 there were 40 employees with sales of 200 million pesetas. A further indication of success was that as a consulting company with local connections and a local image, it made a very attractive prize for foreign investors and multinational consulting companies were making offers to purchase Grupo Audit. In 1995 Grupo Audit became affiliated with HLB International, a federation of consulting companies with offices in ninety countries. This indicates a strong tendency to maintain a world-class standard of service.

MEDITERRANEA: For the new factory that came about from the collaboration of Luis Ferre and the Caixa, each worker was required to invest a half year's salary. The company performed adequately up until 1983, but then it faced a turning point. In that year, two other cooperatives in the region ran into trouble and their chances of survival looked grim. They looked for advice from the consulting group Caixa, and with its aid, they amalgamated with Mediterranea. This merger added new product lines to the company and resulted in a very powerful commercial entity.

By 1992 this worker cooperative had 250 employees and annual sales of over $14 million. Their specially designed products are blown glass, a process that is supported by the newest technology: the fire temperatures are controlled by a sophisticated computer system. All their raw material is recycled from waste glass gathered from the major cities of Spain. Their factory buildings are spacious, modern and well maintained. The administrative offices are in an ultramodern building with futuristic designs and a comfortable conference room seating over a hundred people.

TRYMOBEL: The development of the furniture cooperative Trymobel is of particular interest as a contrast to the Mondragon enterprises. In Mondragon the consultants shun recuperation of private companies in difficulty. All their enterprises begin with a clear commitment by the workers to a model of worker investment and participation. The origin of Trymobel however is a case of a private furniture company on the edge of bankruptcy in 1984 where the workers and management decided to convert to the model of worker ownership.

When this ailing furniture company decided to join the Caixa group in 1984 they gained not only access to capital but also access to expertise and technical support. Immediately their prospects changed. Their sales grew from 1.2 million in 1985 to 4.4 million in 1993. During this time their workforce increased from 29 to 45. The plan for 1994 included computer terminals at each workstation so that the plant would be completely automated.

C: EVOLUTION TO A NEW PHASE

Review: Inspired by clear community ideals in the spirit of Mondragon the Valencia experiment had gone through a variety of phases between 1969 and 1997. From 1969 to 1977, a small group named *Coinser* evolved from the ideal of reforming their society through the provision of economic services in a democratic manner to a new ideal where they would form powerful business corporations which would be both democratically organized and also have a significant economic impact on the Valencia area. Their first enterprise was Covipar, a housing cooperative; the most successful and enduring enterprise was Consum, a grocery chain. From 1978 to 1983, smaller marginal enterprises disappeared and the *Caixa* grew to be the force that united a number of growing community enterprises.

Crisis and Resolution. Between 1983 and 1988, difficulties and stress arose because of differences in philosophy and strategy among the various participants. More cooperatives and small businesses began to use the services provided and more new people became involved. The idea was that enterprises would not only become financial clients but also members of an economic movement dedicated to community improvement.

As R. M. Verdu points out in his authoritative history of the Valencia experiment, a crisis gradually arose in this period:

> In the experience of the *Caixa Popular*, cooperatives joined for a diversity of reasons, often divergent,...and sometimes reducible to obtaining financial resources and consulting services - many were not able to accept and assume the converse responsibilities as an associate of the group... this lack of full commitment to the group is closely related with the loss of autonomy involved in associating with a larger group, and this goes against the desire for independence by many cooperatives which is a continual danger in the inter-cooperative experience.[2]

Because of confusion and lack of clear commitment, the Caixa found itself helping a significant number of cooperatives which refused to reciprocate by doing all of their business with the Caixa. They were willing to take from the central group but they were not willing to give back. Between 1984 and 1987 there was little common focus among the members of the Caixa. There were no common shared economic projects and no common strategies to guide the individual enterprises. In 1988 after a great deal of discussion the key leaders decided to invite a delegation from Mondragon to lead a seminar entitled: "Group Cooperativism and the Experience of the Group of Cooperatives linked to the Credit Union Caixa Popular." The result of that seminar was the formation of a new structure GECV, in the following year, 1989 and the beginning of a new phase of development.

The Cooperative Entrepreneurial Group of Valencia (GECV).

In 1988 the leaders invited those uncommitted cooperatives and associated businesses within their group to decide whether they wished to participate fully or not. A new entity was incorporated the next year under the name "El Grup Empresarial Cooperativ Valencia" (GECV for short). GECV became the Valencia equivalent of the Congress in Mondragon. As Verdu terms it, they allowed the uncommitted cooperatives to "liberate themselves from the yoke of the group."[3] GECV members share a common vision, share resources and develop common strategies for development in the Valencia area. Beyond a concern for survival of each as an entity they act as a development agent for the Valencia community and thus like to call themselves, "The Entrepreneurial Group." Although the official members numbered only nine key cooperative enterprises, each continues to do business with a wide variety of clients, both cooperative and non-cooperative. In its annual statement the Caixa is very clear in its mandate:

> In the Caixa Popular, the primordial concern is efficiency of management, as well as the fulfilment of a basic social role. Caixa Popular holds as a corporate philosophy the support for and identification with the values of participation, solidarity between businesses and preoccupation with the environment, which can make us engines of wealth development for our Valencian community.[4]

By 1996, the GECV group of community-cooperative enterprises had grown to eleven with a combined asset base of $70,000 million pesetas ($700 million Canadian).

Summary: Beginning with the group of activists in Coinser, the community cooperative enterprises have evolved into a strong, united group of eleven community businesses. Five of these are worker cooperatives, four are mixed cooperatives, one is a joint stock company and one is a cooperative group.

GECV Group of Community-Cooperative Enterprises

Worker cooperatives: (5)
La Mediterranea (glass and ceramics)
Florida (university level college)
Marti Sorolla (primary school)
Grupo Audit (accounting and business consulting)
Trymobel (furniture factory)

Mixed groups with client as well as worker-members: (4)
Caixa Popular (credit union or community bank)
Consum (a retail chain)
Assecoop (an insurance company)
Comismar (social service)

Joint Stock Company with employee shareholders: (1)
Foradia Over forty years old; specializes in machine tools,
technical maintenance and repair.

Recent housing development group: (1)
Formedia Housing Development Cooperative started up in 1995.

Since the GECV or Entrepreneurial Group was formed in 1988, growth has been strong and steady.

Year	1989	1993	1995	1996
Employees	1,379	2,403	2,809	3,808
Sales	$154 mil.*	$477 mil.	$590 mil.	$716 mil.
Profits	$3 mil.	$6 mil.	$11.6 mil.	$11 mil.

*Canadian funds.
Figures from Annual Report - 1996.

D: THE FUTURE OF THE VALENCIA EXPERIMENT

Leaders in the Valencia experiment are very conscious of competitive pressure in the new Europe. They know that they are competent in what they do but they can't rest on their oars. Already, some well established multinational companies have attempted to buy them out. However, they have remained loyal to their original dedication to development in their own home area. Thus they have chosen a strategy to seek alliances with other like-minded commercial entities. At the present time, the Grupo Audit, their consulting arm, is associated with the consulting groups of Mondragon. At the same time, Consum has a commercial agreement with Eroski of Mondragon. When asked the reason for these moves, the general manager of Consum answered with one word: "Survival."

Locally, the group is strengthening the GECV structure and is open to new members who are ready to make a serious commitment to collaboration and sharing of resources. New members can become part of the core group of GECV even though not cooperatives in the traditional sense. Some will be share-capital companies in which workers own the majority of shares. GECV leaders are not dogmatic about that sort of thing, and are more concerned with the philosophical and commercial orientation of the company. They seek allies to help them create a strong, significant structure that will bring about local economic development in a manner that is morally and socially responsible.

I have used the term "experiment" in speaking of both the Mondragon and the Valencia groups. In their history and in their attitude, the Mondragon Experiment and the Valencia Experiment are committed to constant experimentation and change. When asked what they will do in three or four years, they often admit that they don't know. In contrast to community-initiated movements in other countries, they have shown a tremendous flexibility and readiness to loosen their structures and reform them. Rather than being inflexibly committed to one structure or even to one idea, they adapt to new circumstances and this manifests a tremendous loyalty to their employees and the local communities where their employees live.

E: BASIC PRINCIPLES

As in the case of Mondragon, the Valencia group tends to assess and reorganize frequently. Also, in Valencia there is a key group of core leaders who grew with the system. The constant leader has been Josep Soriano Besso and his close colleagues who have moved from one organization to the other within the system. In addition the core group has concerned itself with much more than simply creating new businesses. They have aspired to create new *community-oriented* businesses which incorporate certain principles and qualities.

Rosario M. Verdu whose book is the official history of the Valencia group, points out some of these guidelines or principles. [5]

1. ***Capitalization*** This means that no profits are taken out. All surpluses are reinvested for expansion and development which translates into new jobs for the community.

2. ***Salary Equity*** Salary differences are limited in a "3 to 1" ratio.

3. ***Professionalization of Management*** All member enterprises must seek and choose the best qualified managers possible.

4. ***Planning*** All member enterprises must prepare both a short-term and a long-term plan.

5. ***Management Control*** Management must have a control system in place, although this is counter-balanced by Principle #6.

6. ***Co-Responsibility*** This encourages worker participation in all aspects of the enterprise.

7. ***Representation*** All members have the right to vote.

8. ***Management Openness*** The books as well as the door must be open.

9. ***Economic Cooperation*** Must exist between Cooperative Enterprises for development and creation of new enterprises.

10. ***Formation*** Employee education and development.

11. ***Philosophy of Development*** which promotes:
    a) the cooperative enterprise as instrument for community development
    b) political neutrality
    c) ethical behaviour

Some key elements in the Mission Statements are:
1. Develop a cooperative group of enterprises which are expansionist but, nevertheless, viable, efficient, dynamic and reformist.
2. Create stable employment through maintaining and creating cooperative businesses which are capable of creating jobs for the future.
3. Increase the stability of the member enterprises by favouring structural improvements, institutional support, inter-cooperative linkages and an articulated philosophy.

Beyond the importance of expressions of community solidarity and community concern, Valencia is important because it is another empirical example of a community-motivated commercial enterprise which is successful in business terms. Initiated in 1969, the Valencia experiment has already proven itself and is still growing. The key instrumental elements of technology, finance and formation are present and they are directed by a strong sense of mission based on communal values.

The cooperative community business movements in Mondragon and Valencia arose out of the same concern that stimulated social economic initiatives in North America. Community people became concerned about their economic well-being and organized themselves to make their local society a better place in which to live. These are exercises in human and community solidarity. They are concrete expressions of the belief that we are all one family and that we have a duty to each other.

Notes

1. George Orwell described this situation in his *Homage to Catalonia*, London: Secker and Warburg, 1951.
2. Rosario Martinez Verdu, *El Grup Empresarial Cooperativ Valencia,* Valencia: Grup Empresarial, 1990, p. 103.
3. *Ibid.*, p.105.
4. Annual Report, 1993, Caixa Popular, p. 3.
5. Verdu, *op. cit.*, p. 67.

CHAPTER 7

NORTH AMERICAN GLIMMERINGS

While there is no experiment in the Americas that comes close to the integrated systems of Mondragon and Valencia, there is a sound basis for hope. First of all, there is the sleeping giant of the cooperative movement.[1] Most people are not aware of the size and extent of cooperative business in the Western World. In Canada alone, credit unions, our cooperative banks, have a total asset base of over 90 billion dollars. This is an enormous force. Beyond the credit unions, the annual revenues of the other cooperatives is over 22 billion. This includes a wide variety such as consumer stores, insurance, marketing, fishing co-ops and the wheat pools. Most Canadians belong to one sort of cooperative or another. Nevertheless this huge conglomerate has been vastly underutilized and underdeveloped as a force for economic change. In spite of the visionary pioneers, the movement has become a system dedicated to a more narrowly defined service function in contrast to the Mondragon community business approach that accepts the mission of generalized community economic development.

My interest here concerns community business initiatives which show some potential for evolution in the Mondragon sense. The cases are diverse and are meant to illustrate the diversity of structures and projects that can spring from the same kind of concern that triggered the Mondragon development. I consider this chapter as somewhat of a sharing of experiences and observations.

While recognizing that there are wonderful examples in the United States, I will limit this section to Canada, especially the East Coast, and one small area in Mexico. Concerning Canada, I merely outline a few examples with which I am familiar.[2] Each case I have selected appears to be a seedling with the potential to blossom into a more comprehensive community business corporation. As Professor Schweickart pointed out in the letter quoted in chapter one, the global market place is not friendly to this type of business. He says that "capitalism will never be brought down by some process of peaceful, fair competition with worker-owned firms. Because the competition will never be fair. Not when capitalism can scour the world for low wages and compliant governments." This is a dark picture indeed. But, instead of cursing the darkness of little progress in the field of community economic development, we can see these North American initiatives as candles offering us hope.

A. COMMUNITY BUSINESS CORPORATIONS

I use the term "community business corporation" to indicate a class of business that is specifically set up for the purpose of improving the local community and creating jobs. This is in contradistinction to corporations which have been organized for the main purpose of creating dividends for shareholders. I have no intention of making a blanket judgement concerning such conventional companies. I simply wish to point out the necessity of organizing new kinds of business corporations to perform the task that the conventional, dominant corporations do not, and perhaps cannot do. The key characteristic of a community business corporation is that it looks for business opportunities which are clearly good for the local community and which are commercially viable. They are multifunctional or multisectoral, which distinguishes them from most cooperatives, which are usually unifunctional. The range and variety that exists are here indicated by four examples from Atlantic Canada, one from northern Saskatchewan and two from British Columbia.

New Dawn. One case is New Dawn Enterprises in Cape Breton.[3] It was established in the early 1970s by local citizens concerned about local economic decline. In response to the expressed needs of the community, New Dawn established a large real-estate portfolio offering affordable housing for people on low and medium income as well as a home for the aged, dental centres and a wide variety of job-creation schemes. The total assets are now over $14 million. New Dawn itself is a not-for-profit mother corporation with a number of subsidiaries. The mere fact that a community corporation like New Dawn has survived over twenty-five years should indicate that serious business can be undertaken in an efficient manner even though it is for community good rather than the financial profit of the board, a few individuals or any one special interest group.

Although the founders of New Dawn began by using the American term "Community Development Corporation,"[4] the inspiration and source did not come from the United States. The organizers were active in a number of organizations including cooperatives, credit unions, labour, senior citizen groups and business. All admired the cooperative movement and identified with the local tradition of self help in economic development. However, the originators were clear in their conclusion that traditional cooperative forms were too rigid and that a new and more flexible formula was necessary. As long as community purpose and one vote per person were maintained, they didn't worry about changing other aspects of the cooperative concept.

New Dawn never saw itself as serving any one special interest group such as consumers, producers or employees. The board saw itself as serving the community interest in general and relied heavily on volunteer input. Some people volunteered to join and others were recruited. In a sense, New Dawn's board is formed along lines similar to that of a hospital or of a university. The board, committees and the volunteer resource centre involved approximately two hundred people in New Dawn in 1995.

Inquirers are often surprised when they learn how simple it was to start New Dawn as a business. The board members signed a bank guarantee and borrowed $20,000 in 1973. (Credit unions were not involved in business loans at that time.) New Dawn then bought an old run-down building and fixed it up through grants and volunteer labour. Based on the increased equity, more properties were bought and new projects initiated. The intention to make money was explicit, but as a means and not as an end. When profit was made on one project, the money was used to expand into new commercial areas. The basic rule is that each project must serve some community need and must pay its own way. If it cannot, it will close, no matter how wonderful the idea. For example, New Dawn started a business to sell and clean healthy, ecological baby diapers. However, it lost money so it was closed down very quickly.

In 1989, Dr. Rankin MacSween, a former professor at the University College of Cape Breton, became the executive director of New Dawn. By 1997, the staff had exceeded 100 with a payroll of over $1.7 million. Without the help of any government grants, New Dawn is now clearly self-sustaining. Within the private-community sector it functions as a flexible business structure, able to respond to a variety of community needs.

An example of a New Dawn initiative occurred with the closing down of the Department of Defence radar base in Cape Breton in 1990. A wide variety of unsuccessful efforts were made to utilize the vacant facility. Eventually local government authorities approached New Dawn because it was the only organized institution in the area able to take over such a facility. New Dawn agreed to acquire the property and developed it as a housing and business complex. This particular military establishment contained sixty residential units, mostly duplex homes. With a good sense of social entrepreneurship New Dawn has turned the majority of these lodgings into home-care units for the aged. Three senior citizens are lodged in one side and a family is lodged in the other. The family is paid a fee to care for the three seniors. The benefits are far-reaching. The seniors are kept out of the large nursing homes, people are given jobs in an area of high unemployment and New Dawn makes a bit of money from the project.

Colville. Nanaimo, on Vancouver island, has some connections with Cape Breton Island. During the depression of the late 1920s coal-miners from Cape Breton went to the Nanaimo region looking for work. The Nanaimo area, including a town called Colville, subsequently suffered some of the effects of a declining resource-based economy. Colville provides a very interesting historical example concerning Canadian federal job creation strategy since the mid 1970s. While names of government departments change and names of programs change, there is a clear continuity by the federal "Manpower-Employment-Human Resource" Department of a string of similar programs called LIP, LEAP, LEADA, BDC and, more recently, Community Futures. The concept generally includes a contribution by the department to a community based committee which is to hire staff and lend money to small local businesses.

Originally organized as "Central Island Community Development Society" the Colville group concentrated on the government programs which provided training for the unemployed. Led by Don MacMillan, their executive director, they sought to develop a strategy with more accent on development of businesses as a way of creating jobs. A big boost for the Colville group came in 1975 when they received a one time grant of $500,000 for local investment. With the help of this grant, the group set up a subsidiary called Colville Investment Corporation to manage the fund.

In subsequent years this Nanaimo-based group continued to operate under the various formulations of federal Employment Department programs. Federal support provided annual capital grants and funds to enable staff to carry on various training and advisory tasks for the local community. Importantly, the group provided continuity. Besides providing many local companies with technical assistance, the Colville group, as of 1994, was responsible for creating 1,622 jobs in the business sector and 820 jobs in the non-profit community sector. Between 1975 and 1994 the Colville Investment Corporation loaned out $7.7 million to small businesses. This role of lending has become increasingly critical in the 1990s because, in many such communities, the commercial banks refuse to make small business loans unless the loan is guaranteed by third party sources or through liens on personal assets of the borrower.

Many of the government supported community loan programs in Canada have been passive. Having received federal capital for loans, most groups tended to wait for applicants to apply. In contrast, this Nanaimo group has taken a pro-active stance from the first. With the half million dollar grant in 1975, they took a variety of initiatives to organize local development projects such as:

    i.   spearheading the development of an adult-learning centre,

    ii. developing the basis for targeted training and support for young people becoming involved in business,

    iii. creating a partnership with the local credit union to jointly finance certain projects and to sell Colville's mature loans in order to recycle capital (one project jointly financed with the Credit Union is a company to manufacture solar-powered gondolas for marine based tourism.)

    iv. a neighbourhood revitalization program for a section of town in serious decline.[5]

All across Canada there have been cases of government grants to large companies which went bankrupt with amounts of government subsidy being lost ranging from $1 million to $100 million dollars. The federal subsidy given to this Nanaimo group is negligible in comparison. It is an example of how a modest federal contribution can trigger a local community-based corporation that will become self-sustaining and an active agent for development in the long term.

Revelstoke. Another creative British Columbia initiative, the Revelstoke Enterprise Centre, was formed as part of a community response to the loss of 1,200 jobs when the Revelstoke dam construction was completed.What is particularly striking about this initiative is the level of interagency cooperation that has been established. A variety of organizations have clubbed together to develop a joint approach to development. The concrete manifestation of this attitude is the sharing of one building by Community Futures, the Chamber of Commerce, the Business Development Centre and the Economic Development Commission. Usually such groups compete with each other and rarely share the same office infrastructure. Their combined staff of sixty-one is a powerful force when directed to local development.

Through such a joint approach this group has been successful in a number of areas such as:

- a $2.8 million restoration program in 1986, funded in part by a municipal tax increase voted by the residents.
- a Maritime Railway Museum.
- a Community Forest Corporation which now owns and manages a tree farm license. With the support of local saw-mill operators, the municipality also voted to assist this initiative.

HRDA. The Human Resources Development Association (HRDA) in Halifax, Nova Scotia, is a different kind of example of how government dollars can be put to creative and useful development. It is mainly funded through welfare dollars. In 1978, Harold Crowell, the director of social services for the city, convinced city and provincial officials to go along with his plan to take people off the welfare rolls and put them to work. With an agreement to use $275,000 from the city welfare budget, Crowell and the officials organized a board to manage HRDA. Through this plan, new businesses were set up to train and employ welfare recipients who were willing to participate. Since it is voluntary, there are no penalties for social assistance recipients not wishing to participate.

Over the years the HRDA has undertaken a wide variety of business ventures. Used domestic appliances were refurbished and sold, a rent-a-wreck car rental franchise was undertaken and a commercial cleaning service was set up. While they dropped some businesses such as the car rental agency and took on others such as a recycling plant, the idea has always been the same: use welfare dollars for training and job creation through businesses that will eventually become self-sustaining.

HRDA has a built-in stability because the city and the province have agreed to a support plan. According to the agreement, for every person HRDA removes from the welfare list, the city will pay 50% of the cost of the wages on a monthly basis for up to one year. Analysts have estimated that for every dollar invested in HRDA by government, two dollars returns to the treasury through various taxes.

Great Northern Peninsula Development Corporation (GNP). Of all the areas in Canada that appear to have little reason for hopeful initiative, Newfoundland/Labrador stands out because of its northern isolation and the near shutdown of the fishing industry. The Great Northern Peninsula Development Corporation (GNPDC) was set up in 1987. It is remarkable that within a short time, this group, familiarly called GNP, has been able to initiate business ventures worth over one million dollars. Of special interest is the fact that the "new" commercial complex grew out of the previously existing social organizations in the local area. There was no importing of a high powered outside corporation. They built on what was already there.

The Great Northern Peninsula stretches north, above Deer Lake, for approximately 500 kilometres and almost touches Labrador. The population of approximately 26,000 is widely dispersed. St. Anthony is the largest centre with 2,000 people while most villages average two or three hundred inhabitants.

Although they did start in fishery production, GNP built flexibility into their initial structure, so that when the fishery failed they were able to move to forestry, crafts and aquaculture. This multi-functional structure was crucial to GNP's survival. Without it, GNP would have disappeared with the decline of the fishing industry.

GNP's most successful venture was a response to the construction of a wood-chip generating station. GNP quickly set up a joint venture company called Northchip with GNP owning 51 per cent of the shares and six small sawmill operators owning 49 per cent. The corporation prepared all the technical plans and negotiated a package of grants and bank loans. Each sawmill operator invested from five thousand to twenty-five thousand dollars. In 1988 a four year contract for $4.8 million was awarded to GNP. It had the lowest price over outside competitors. The amount required to launch this company was close to one million dollars. Various wood-chipping machines and trailers were purchased; the task of hauling the chips was contracted out to a local trucking company. The financial package was developed with the assistance of the Atlantic Canada Opportunities Agency (ACOA) which is the main federal development arm in the region. David Simms, the founding president, has promoted a spirit of innovation and expansion, travelling as far as Iceland for new techniques.

The future of this subsidiary company is optimistic. GNP has expanded into other areas such as the selling of lumber and wood products for both the domestic and export market. During 1993, the small-scale sawmill members decided to collaborate on the development of one common sawmill with up-to-date technology. In 1997, Northchip made an agreement with a company in New Brunswick to distribute its products. Northchip is now the optimistic flagship of GNP. The company is also looking at the possibility of providing heat from wood-chips for a local school. From the first GNP has been conscious of the importance of good technology and research. They are intensely involved in various experimental aquaculture projects, such as raising arctic char and mussels, and are examining possibilities of using the warmed water from a thermal generating plant. In the shrimp fishery they have also been instrumental in the introduction of a special sorting grate to reduce damage to other species. In the craft area they have developed a variety of uses for adult seal-skin. With a total budget of some $3 million, GNP is well on the way to long-term self-sufficiency.

Evangeline. Prince Edward Island is one of the more dynamic centres for local development in the region. There are three active business development centres, part of the federal Community Futures Program, as well as other community economic projects sponsored by a range of groups such as the Royal Canadian Legion Branch 26 in Morell. However, the most fascinating example is located in the Evangeline area.

The Evangeline group of cooperatives in Prince Edward Island exemplifies the principle of collaboration and inter-linkage to achieve economic development. Located in the small communities of Wellington, Mount Carmel and Abram's Village, it serves a total population of approximately 2,500 people within a 20 square kilometre area. In this area of very high unemployment, approximately 369 people are employed in a broad range of activities which include: a mall with supermarket, a funeral cooperative, a credit union, a fishing cooperative, a forestry project, a senior citizen's home, a cablevision service and a youth cooperative. In the tourism sector they have developed the "Acadian Pioneer Village" which includes a hotel, a restaurant and a theatre as well as handicrafts.

The revenue for this cooperative consortium was $4.8 million in 1989-90 with assets over $23 million. A key to success has been the credit union which served as a financial agent under the leadership of Leonce Bernard. In their own way the group used the Mondragon principle of capturing local funds for local development and the notion of using one successful business as a springboard to get another started. In some ways Evangeline is similar to New Dawn in that it is multi-functional with an orientation towards the creation of new community enterprises.[6]

La Ronge Indigenous Initiative. In Northern Saskatchewan, the La Ronge First Nation Band formed the Kitsaki Development Corporation (KDC) in 1981. It is a limited company owned by the band and given the specific mandate to create jobs in this area where the unemployment rates are typically over 80%. The band itself has 5,500 members scattered in small communities stretching 300 kilometres from North to South. Realizing their technical limitations, they adopted a strategy of joint venturing, which is really another way of achieving technology transfer. They joined forces with companies that had more expertise than they did.

By 1992 KDC had received approximately $1.3 of capital from federal sources and used it to attract over $43 million in investment capital. With $18 million in annual revenues they are now able to generate enough profit to cover all operating costs. Through their joint venturing strategy they are involved in: processing and marketing dried meat products and wild rice, services such as insurance and funerals, trucking, a motor hotel and various services to mining companies. They have created 500 jobs, half of which are held by aboriginal people.

B. ALTERNATIVE FINANCIAL INITIATIVES

Within the field of community economic development there is a new consciousness concerning the importance of capital in any serious effort to bring about social and economic reform. Governments have recognized this through a variety of programs from Community Futures to the Saskatchewan Community Bonds and the Ontario Community Investment Shares. Following are five examples of community groups who are evolving a variety of alternative financial initiatives: one each in New Brunswick, Quebec and Ontario, and two from Nova Scotia.

Mouvement Coopératif Acadien. In New Brunswick, the strongest current for community economic development appears to be in the Acadian regions, especially in the Northeast area, where the unemployment levels are highest. The Acadian communities have organized their own New Brunswick cooperative organization called *"Mouvement Coopératif* Acadien" (MCA)[7]. The MCA is made up of 130 cooperative organizations including thirteen hundred volunteers and three thousand employees. In 1996, the Acadian credit unions of New Brunswick exceeded $1.5 billion in assets. It is quite clear that the most powerful organizations for community economic development in New Brunswick are under the umbrella of the cooperative movement. While the English speaking cooperatives tend to be unifunctional and service oriented, the Acadian cooperatives see themselves as agents for social and economic change. They tend to be much more adventurous and non-traditional as is indicated in the following example.

In 1990, a number of Acadian cooperative groups in Caraquet decided to play a more active role in the struggle against unemployment. A series of meetings and discussions were held amongst the major cooperative organizations in the area led by the well known cooperative leaders, Raymond Gionet and Gilles Menard. The result was a new venture finance company comprising the following partners:

1. The Acadian Credit Unions of New Brunswick
2. The Acadian Cooperative Stores of New Brunswick
3. The Acadian Credit Union Insurance Company
4. Co-op Atlantic
5. The Federal Government
6. The Provincial Government

Incorporated in December, 1990, the new venture finance company was named *La Societé d'Investissement du Mouvement Acadien (SIMA).* The provincial government boosted the organization's initiative by providing a $1 million interest free loan for seven years. Another $1.6 million was provided by various cooperatives and credit unions to attain an asset base of $2.6 million by the end of 1992. The objective of the fund is to finance local business development and job creation. Some of the clients are cooperatives and some are individual and privately owned businesses. The important thing is that they are businesses which are locally owned and locally controlled and the jobs and profits stay in the local area. It is a clear manifestation of the intention of cooperative leaders in this region to assume a role of leadership in solving their local economic problems.

By December of 1992, SIMA had invested $357,000 in five companies. Most of this was in the form of share capital. The clients were: a printing business, a maple sugar cooperative, a funeral cooperative, a natural food cooperative and a blueberry packing plant. Besides providing capital, SIMA also provides advice and technical assistance to client companies. Client companies must also be willing to allow SIMA delegates to sit on their boards.

The investment policy of SIMA contains a number of restrictions reminiscent of Mondragon principles. They are:

1. client companies must be local with their headquarters in New Brunswick
2. they must have growth potential
3. they must have at least three partner-owners
4. they must encourage employees to invest in the company
5. they must use the investment money to generate growth
6. SIMA may not purchase more than 30 per cent of the shares nor invest more than $200,000 in any one company.
7. SIMA will not invest in any company in which one person owns more than 70 per cent of the shares.

Solidarité. Quebec abounds with examples of social-economic experimentation. Besides the credit unions of the *"Mouvement Desjardins"* which is as large as any private bank in that province, Quebec leads in labour-union based investment funds. The best known and most successful is called "Solidarity." Through worker investments which receive tax credits, the fund now totals approximately one billion dollars. Founded by a major labour union congress, the Quebec Federation of Labour, the objective of Solidarity is "to encourage the development of Quebec business enterprises by inviting labour to participate in such development by subscribing to shares of the Fund."[8] Dedicated to the preservation of jobs in Quebec, Solidarity invests in both union and non-union businesses. With a staff of 30 financial analysts, Solidarity takes a pro-active role and appoints board members to client companies. They are very flexible and undogmatic in their investments. For instance, they invested five million dollars in the Expo Baseball team in order to keep it in the province. Following the example of Quebec, most other provinces are putting in place legislation to encourage similar venture capital funds.

Quebec is also the province with the most worker-owned businesses. Besides regular worker cooperatives which are totally owned by workers, Quebec is promoting, through legislation, a new kind of hybrid called the "worker shareholder cooperative." In this model, a conventional company sells a portion of its shares to the employees who form a cooperative to own the shares jointly. It differs from typical U.S. style ESOPs (employee stock ownership programs) in which the workers do not have their own board members. In the case of the Quebec model, workers do have board representatives and do participate in key management decisions. For example, the employees' cooperative owns one third of the shares in the Sacre Coeur sawmill. Also in ACG Jeans, the employees formed a cooperative to buy 30 percent of the shares and they have board representation. In 1994, there were approximately fifty worker-shareholder cooperatives in Quebec.

Algoma. In Ontario the most famous example of corporate experimentation is Algoma Steel. Located in Sault Ste. Marie, a city of 80,000, this steel plant was scheduled for closure in 1990. As Canada's third largest steelmaker, employing approximately 6,000 workers, this industry was of strategic importance for the surrounding communities. Through the leadership of the United Steelworkers of America, representing the workers, a joint plan was worked out. It involved the Ontario government, the former owners, and the steel union. The process began to take serious shape when, at the request of the steel union, the provincial government set up a task force in May of 1991. In August, the community formed a local corporation called "Algoma Community Action Team" to involve the broader community. Within a short time, 22,000 residents of the city contributed $165,000 to the fund.

Eventually a plan was worked out for what was to be the biggest worker buy-out in Canada. As part of the plan, both workers and management took a reduction in wages which were converted into equity shares in the new steel company. Also they agreed to a reduction in the 6,000 person workforce by 1,600 over a five year period, if necessary. After negotiation and discussion, a company structure was finally established. The employees obtained 60% of the shares of the new company. These shares, representing the value of the agreed-upon wage reductions, were turned over to a trust. The other forty percent of the shares were purchased by private investors. The employees then organized a cooperative and through this structure they received voting shares which gave them authority over four company issues:

1. the sale of the company,
2. investments by Algoma outside of their community,
3. any major operating change by the company not approved by eight board members,
4. and the issuance of stock that would dilute the employees stock below fifty per cent.

The board of directors of Algoma is made up of thirteen members: four chosen by the Steelworkers, one chosen by management staff and seven independents who are acceptable to the unions, the other stakeholders and the CEO. Besides sitting on the board, the employees participate on many levels. Through a Joint Steering Committee, they have established special task forces for such purposes as: Cost Reduction, Workplace Redesign and Technology, and Worker Training.

Outside of Quebec this is the only worker-shareholder cooperative in Canada. In this case, the cooperative members also happen to be labour union members. The cooperative structure and the labour union structure are closely intertwined, with the national president of the International Steelworkers Union, or his delegate, serving automatically as chairperson of the cooperative. Through this complex structure the workers are guaranteed a real role in the operation of the company. For instance, the chief executive officer is chosen by a joint labour-management search committee.

From a Mondragon perspective, Algoma is the community oriented business with the greatest potential in all of English-speaking Canada. In 1994, they made over $100 million in profits. This kind of commercial success allows options not available to small-scale fledgling community businesses. In a sense there are two possibilities for Algoma. One is that the main concern will be internal: protecting the jobs of employees. Then it will simply be a successful steel plant. The other possibility is that it will turn outwards in an attempt to help the other unemployed people in the area. In the latter case it could be the key building block to transform the Sault region with a new consortium of community owned businesses in the Mondragon spirit.

BCA (Acronym for Banking Community Assets). In the mid-nineteen eighties, some members of New Dawn saw the increasing need for the development of a capital pool to help implement new ventures. Out of their discussions, and with the help of the Community Economic Development Institute at the University College of Cape Breton, they eventually set up a study group. After consulting with diverse experts in the field of finance and conducting protracted negotiations with related institutions such as the Credit Union Central and Cooperators Insurance, the group finally decided to take the plunge on their own. They formed a legal entity called "BCA Holdings Ltd." This new enterprise was organized to raise money in the community to be used to help old and new small businesses. The idea was readily supported because most business people found that the regular banks were not prepared to take risks in areas of high unemployment. A great opportunity presented itself to the group in 1990. The local federal development agency, Enterprise Cape Breton Corporation, had offered an interest-free loan of one half million dollars to the Board of Trade, to be used as a venture development fund, if the Board could match that amount. When the Board declined, considering that it was outside their mandate, the BCA group took up the challenge. BCA argued that it is most appropriate for government agencies to partner with community-based not-for-profit community business groups.

Within one year, BCA had raised one half million dollars in the local community and began business with a one million dollar fund. Of course the total amount was in the form of a loan which had to be repaid. The government money was interest free for five years, but the community investors were paid 5 per cent interest. New Dawn and New Deal Development Corporation, with headquarters in Sydney Mines, provided loan guarantees which were very important in providing BCA with financial muscle. With a volunteer board, this not-for-profit company achieved some rapid successes. Four investment examples illustrate how a relatively small amount of money can have a very significant effect in a depleted community.

1. *Tompkins Commercial Centre:* The small, local credit union needed a new building, but could not afford it. A joint venture was proposed by BCA. A joint non-profit company was set up. Although it had no money, the new company had good will and community support. With some interest-free loans from credit unions in the mining towns and loan capital from BCA, a building worth half a million dollars was built as a kind of mini-mall. Owned by the new company, "Tompkins Development Ltd.," the building at

tracted a number of tenants. The anchor tenant was Tim
Horton's Donuts while the other tenants were the Reserve
Mines Credit Union, the Regional Library and a credit union museum sponsored by the Nova Scotia Credit Union
Central. Rent from the tenants will pay off the mortgage
and at that point this community business corporation will
have a strong asset base to do other things.

2. *East Coast Rope.* When a rope company in the area went
bankrupt in 1992 a large corporation from Louisiana quickly
moved in, purchased the machinery from the receivers, and
tried to ship it out. The local community was enraged since
over three million dollars of government subsidy had gone
into the company. BCA led the way to set up a new company called "East Coast Rope." Outside investors were
recruited in a kind of joint venture approach, with majority
control remaining local. Because of the community force
and provincial support, the U.S. company had to retreat.
One year later, management was delighted with the high
quality and strength of the rope being produced. Upwards
of 26 people are being employed on a 24 hour basis. There
is hope that a strong relationship with the University College of Cape Breton will help to implement a worker development strategy, a strong Research and Development
program and a marketing campaign. The company will seriously look at new products based upon high strength fibre
production. Local business shareholders are devoting a lot
of volunteer time to the development of this company. In
1995 the company was selling 30 per cent of its product in
British Columbia.

3. *Plumbing and Heating.* In a period of frequent bankruptcies the role of BCA in reconstituting a company in plumbing and heating has been a great success. BCA provided
the capital which the banks had refused to do. The new
company, A&B Mechanical, did not miss one payment and
has an overloaded order-book.

4. *Hotel.* A small hotel in St. Peters, on the south side of the
Bras d'Or Lakes, was offered for sale through bankruptcy.
For several reasons this small hotel was of strategic impor-
tance. Next to the canal linking the ocean to the Bras d'Or
Lakes, it is centred in a key historical area close to a

Mi'kmaq community. BCA was the successful bidder and is collaborating with the local indigenous community which is working on a plan for development around the concept of eco-tourism. The hotel is now called "Bras d'Or Lakes Inn."

5. *Radio*. In 1994, the last locally owned radio station in the Sydney area went bankrupt. Immediately, a large outside company which already owned two stations in the area, attempted to purchase the station. BCA objected to monopoly control and with strong citizen support, BCA purchased the station. To avoid future bankruptcy, BCA sold a minority interest to a large Halifax radio-chain to manage the station. BCA recognized the need to import professional technology, but BCA appointed an editorial committee. The station became profitable after one year.

Inspired by the Mondragon-Valencia example, the organizers of this community venture finance company, BCA, were confirmed in their conviction that access to local capital is a key element in development. With a capital base of slightly more than one million dollars, and no grants, significant economic projects were triggered in less than two years after the startup in 1991. However, without full-time staff, BCA has not had the resources to develop a strong, social participatory system.

The Crocus Investment Fund of Manitoba is another example of a labour-sponsored venture fund. Initiated by the Manitoba Federation of Labour in 1990, the fund now holds assets of over $50 million. It is supported both the federal and provincial governments and the local business community. Government has provided approximately $4.5 million in various forms of seed capitalization. The fund has been strengthened by institutional investments from groups such as the Manitoba Credit Union Central and the Manitoba Government Employee's Union Strike Fund.

As pointed out in a Crocus document the objectives of the Fund are:

1. To capitalize itself to a level which will permit it to have a significant impact on the Manitoba economy.
2. To educate Manitobans about the consequences of investment decisions and the economic benefits associated with capital retention.
3. To provide a competitive rate of return to the Fund's investors.
4. To foster a range of social policy objectives such as the promotion of ownership by management and employees, as well as participation in corporate governance and management.

This Manitoba example is especially interesting because of the variety of sources from whence support has come—government, labour, business, the cooperative movement and the community at large.

Cape Breton Labourers' Development Corporation. The Cape Breton Labourers' Development Corporation has shown the potential of small amounts of money. Through an ageement with the local of the International Labourers' Union, each member lends 25 cents per hour when employed. They have raised one million dollars in this manner and used this fund to provide interest free mortgages for members in need of housing. They can deliver a house for approximately $300 per month with no down-payment on a twenty year lease-purchase agreement. The union members withdraw their money when they retire. Since 1990 they have built twenty-four houses. If this is possible in an area where the labour union has an unemployment level of 60 percent, imagine what is possible in more prosperous areas. If 1,000 school teachers were to make an interest-free loan pledge of $10 per week, this would total over half a million dollars per year for investment in local job-creation. Further, it is not a gift; it is a loan the teachers will get back when they retire.

Concerning finance, it is remarkable how most poor communities export a tremendous amount of money to wealthier areas. Local people in areas of high unemployment put their money in the regular banks, and the banks accept their money. However, the banks simply will not invest in such areas of economic decline; instead they send the money to the major centres of wealth. It is ironic that poor communities thus export jobs through the banking system. Any community group that is serious about local development must form a locally based investment fund in order to entrap some local capital to be used for job creation and business development. The above examples of alternative financial initiatives illustrate creative Canadian use of the Mondragon principle of entrapping local funds for the good of the local community.

The foregoing brief overview of a few Canadian examples is not intended to be an exhaustive treatment of innovative initiatives in this country. There are many additional ones such as RESO in Montreal (*La Relance Économique du Sud-Oeust de Montréal*), Homes First Society and Carrot Common, both in Toronto, Duffield First Nation Project in Alberta and Vancity Credit Union in Vancouver, but these are already well explained in writings such as *Reinventing the Local Economy* and other community economic development publications.[9]

C. MEXICO: A SUSTAINABLE DEVELOPMENT PROJECT

The case of Mexico is more of a personal adventure. When Mexico joined with Canada and the United States in the North American Free Trade Agreement, there was great excitement in the business communities about the opportunity to "make money" in Mexico. However, history provided a warning, and many of us considered that Canada should not engage in the same harmful kind of relationship to which it was itself subjected in the past. In the nineteenth century, by agreements similar to NAFTA, corporations in England were attracted by the great opportunities in Canada. After exploiting the mineral resources of places like Cape Breton, they departed with their profits and left behind many empty holes in the ground. A great deal of damage was done, socially, economically, environmentally and spiritually. Socially responsible people in Canada feared NAFTA, not so much because of free trade, but rather because of the U.S. political pressure to dismantle the social safety net.

As NAFTA came on stream, a number of Canadians were more interested in the notion of sharing and partnerships with Mexico rather than opportunities for exploitation. Mexico is at a critical juncture in its history. Torn between the "developed" north and the "developing" south, it is drawn by the wealth of the United States, but its heart is in South America. For many such reasons, I considered Mexico an excellent testing ground for some of the ideas discussed above concerning community economic development.

In 1992, I visited the Canadian Embassy in Mexico and asked their advice in finding a community economic development project in an area similar to Cape Breton. More specifically the idea was to find a project in an area near the ocean where there was a significant native population, a university and a depleted economy. That place turned out to be the Yucatan Peninsula. The Yucatan Peninsula resembled Cape Breton Island in at least eleven ways.

1. Both areas are peripheral. Strong economic development going on in powerful central areas of their respective nations causes outmigration and economic depletion in the local area.

2. Both jut out into the Atlantic and were the first areas of contact with the European system.

3. Both have depended upon a resource based economy which is now depleted. Yucatan lost many thousands of jobs dur-

ing the last twenty years in hennequin-hemp industries while Cape Breton lost thousands in coal, fishery and forestry.

4. Both areas claim to have a culture that is distinct from the dominant one. Both are losing their ancient languages. There are many Yucatan songs as there are many Cape Breton songs. Both have a separatist tendency.

5. Both have an ancient aboriginal population that is struggling to maintain identity.

6. Both are minority systems with traditional and outdated technological systems attempting to compete within a dominant system that is more advanced technologically and technocratically.

7. One is on the North of the United States and one is on the South. Both will enter into the Free Trade System which will increase the gap between the metropolitan and non-metropolitan areas.

8. Both have historic sites and/or natural beauty spots that are threatened by industrial development needed for job-creation.

9. Both have unemployment levels of over 30 per cent.

10. In both, the recent trend has been to depend upon imported industries for job creation.

11. In both, there are fledgling but interesting initiatives to create new structures: for example, New Dawn in Cape Breton Island, and Chac Lol in the Yucatan. These kinds of economic structures attempt to tie into the local economy, as distinct from the dominant one which is owned and controlled externally.

As these points demonstrate, it seems that the Yucatan Peninsula in Mexico and Cape Breton Island in Canada, although culturally and economically very distinct, have some interesting parallels which can be useful to study in the context of sustainable development. Further, it can even be claimed that the national structures of both Canada and Mexico have some similarities as federal systems. Both share a fear of cultural and political domination by the USA. Both are swamped by U.S. television. Also both are threatened by economic sanctions (in cases such as Cuba) if they offend the U.S. policy makers.

Of course, Canada is much more advanced in distribution of wealth and in terms of judicial and political systems. In terms of the dynamic and direction of economic development, however, there are some parallels in both of these former colonies. Both are committed to a free-market liberal economy, based on international competitiveness. Both depend on multinational corporations over which they have little or no control. The oil industry, the auto industry, and to some extent, the food industry are examples. A walk through a major supermarket in either country is pretty good evidence of the control in food products.

In Mexico, there is a developing elite in the workforce, people with specialist, technical skills who have comfortable, long term economic security. Meanwhile the large majority of workers are unemployed or working at starvation wages. (The Chiapas revolt sprang out of this enormous imbalance.) Geographically, certain areas such as Mexico City and the border areas close to the U.S. are centres of the new economic wealth while outlying areas like Chiapas and the Yucatan are remnants of the old resource economy. In Canada, we are also developing an elite, highly paid work force on one side, with a growing pool of unemployed and low paid workers on the other. The impact is cushioned in Canada by an excellent social safety net of unemployment insurance, child benefits, a free medical system and old age pensions. If the safety net were stripped away, we might look somewhat like Mexico. Even with the social safety net, Newfoundland, rural Quebec and most of Northern Canada share some of the disadvantages of the Yucatan Peninsula.

The Brundtland Commission of the United Nations placed emphasis on the term "sustainable development." The premise is twofold: first, "development" indicates that we have an obligation to provide a means of livelihood for people through economic development. Second, the term "sustainable" implies that the development must be managed in such a way that that future survival in the physical and social environment would continue to be possible. The north-south parallels listed above become striking when one thinks in terms of sustainable development.[10] For instance, new mines in Peru and the Canadian North will last twenty or thirty years, and during that time they will provide jobs for the local population. However, when the mines close, there will be nothing to support the unemployed miners. Mines have a short life, but an industry based on seal oil in the north, or cedar in the south, could last hundreds of years. These, like tourist attractions, are renewable resources.

Yucape Project

The project I chose is called Chac Lol (Red Flower in Maya) and is a development cooperative located in six villages south of Merida. Merida, the major city of the whole peninsula, with a population of over 500,000, is a colonial city with incredibly well preserved 16th-century buildings. Approximately sixty kilometres to the south are the Chac Lol villages: Ticul, Muna, Opichen, Maxcanu, Santa Cruz and Calcehotok. The Chac Lol Development Cooperative consists of some agricultural plots, a small cottage shoe manufacturing business, a small corn mill and tortilla maker, a tractor to serve the area and a truck to transport goods. The assets of the group in 1992 amounted to approximately $70,000. Sales were approximately $20,000 per year. This was a fascinating case. Over two hundred campesinos were members of the development cooperative and they were anxious to create more jobs for the community. The key animator was Rommel Gonzalez, a former government official who left his government job to work more closely with the community along with his wife Esther.[11]

After a number of discussions, the leaders invited me to set up some system of collaboration. The possibility of trying to duplicate the kind of partnership that exists in Cape Breton between the University College of Cape Breton and community enterprises was quite fascinating. It would be an experiment in technology transfer. The four original partners in Yucape were: University College of Cape Breton, Chapingo University, Chac Lol and BCA Holdings. As the project developed, the University of Yucatan and the National Institute for Anthropology and History as well as Mayab University joined the group. The International Development Research Centre (IDRC) of Canada provided research support for some innovative strategies for development in Mexico.

Context. The campesino economy is agricultural and labour intensive with low rates of literacy. In contrast, the metropolitan centres which dominate North American society have an economy which is post-industrial, information-based, international and highly competitive. The general pattern has been for the non-metropolitan areas to decline. By the year 2000, it is expected that 90 per cent of the population in the USA and Canada will reside in metropolitan areas. The Mexican pattern for urban and rural relationships is similar.

If the trend continues, the impact on the Mexican campesino economy will be devastating. The campesino economy will give way to the new international system. Industrial, high-tech systems will apply to agriculture. These systems are capital intensive and require high levels of knowledge and expertise, which will probably come in the form of experts from outside the region. With no call for the rural labour force, the tendency will be for the campesino population to leave the countryside and come to the metropolitan areas. By 1992 the experience of Mexico City had indicated that this trend has more negative effects than positive ones. Heavily polluted Mexico City already had a population of over twenty-two million.

In November of 1992, delegates from twenty-four NGOs met in the Canadian Embassy to discuss the emerging situation. The following are some of the observations expressed:

> In the economy we see a profound crisis of production, of marketing, of capital and of technology; the visible consequences of this are seen in high levels of unemployment and low salaries. From an economic perspective, we are of the opinion that this situation will become more grave for the majority of the population once the Free Trade Treaty becomes operational with Canada and the United States.

> In Yucatan the hennequin industry is typical of the agricultural crisis. In 1984, 55,000 campesinos worked in this industry; in 1991 there were 37,000; and now [1992] there are 8,000. These economic areas have changed because of the multinational companies which do not employ human labour to any significant degree.

The report pointed out that 90 percent of the rural population manifests some degree of malnutrition. Also, unemployment is extremely high. With NAFTA, changes have been made in the legislation concerning community-owned agricultural land and forests. The report stated:

> We foresee that with the application of the new political economy, only the large agro-businesses will benefit who apply methods of intensive capital, technology and white collar workers, thereby excluding from any benefit a large sector of the population, accelerating the process of rural impoverishment and migration to the cities.[12]

A Case Study

It is not clear what kind of model will work in some rural villages on the Yucatan peninsula where enormous forces that are creating a new kind of social economic system in which there is no role for a significant campesino population. In the context of the above dynamic of social-economic change, the Yucape group made a proposal to develop and test a process to strengthen existing campesino business enterprises and to create new ones. The long-range purpose, since Mexico will become a close partner with Canada, was to share with some colleagues in Mexico in a common search for a better way to do business.

The immediate purpose was communal and human development, with profit only as a means to an end. Through personal involvement with New Dawn and BCA Holdings as well as through the study of the Mondragon and Valencia experiments, I came to hold the thesis that, in these depleted campesino communities, it is possible "to devise 'intentional' business corporations of an economically significant size." This thesis seemed reasonable as an operating guideline. Normally we are told that the modern business corporation is driven only by market forces with the sole purpose of making profit. On the contrary, New Dawn, Mondragon and most of the cases mentioned above, are driven by an intention to serve the local community. The hypothesis of using profit as a means to such an end is shared by many people. What they still look for is clear proof that it is possible for "community purpose" business corporations to survive on a large scale over a long period of time in America. Yucape may yet prove that it can be done.

The Yucape strategic model includes universities as agents of technology transfer. The underlying development theory presumes that both technological innovation and social innovation are necessary for the social-economic survival of such communities. Governments tend to think that a technological fix will cure problems, while community activists tend to think that good intentions and democratic participation are enough. It is now quite clear that one cannot work without the other. Blind technology that follows only free market forces can destroy societies, while highly ideological movements, without the powers of technology, will be humanly interesting but will remain marginal to the main economy.

Although Chac Lol began in 1989, our joint Canadian-Mexican Yucape project only began in 1994 with the help of a research grant from the International Development Research Centre in Ottawa. With the ideas of Mondragon and Valencia in mind the local leaders and I set up a team to review the structures of Chac Lol. Our basic strategy was twofold:

1. Internally, the project would reinforce structures to encourage local self sufficiency in food production and to provide a kind of buffer against outside market forces. Thus, the improvement of agricultural methods, corn processing and retail shops would become a goal.

2. Externally, new businesses were considered necessary to bring in new money and new jobs. However, we wanted

only those kinds of new businesses which would be culturally and environmentally friendly.

Fundamentally we used the three sided Mondragon triangle of Technology, Formation and Finance as guide. For formation and technology we
relied upon the universities, using notions of technology-transfer which are
commonly accepted in Canada. Chapingo University specializes in agricultural engineering. Their people sought new kinds of production based upon
the land. Above the door of their regional campus is written: "Exploit the
Land, Not People." Also, if we were to respect the Mayan culture it was
important to have specialists involved who understood the cultural context.
Thus we were quite fortunate in enlisting the School of Architecture of the
University of Yucatan, the business department of Mayab University and
the National Institute for History and Archeology.

The Consulting Company. Before very long it became obvious that
a structure was necessary to channel information. For this, we set up a
consulting company called CAIPARU. The key members were mainly the
people who were already involved with Chac Lol. Next, a small loan fund
was set up *(fondo revolvente)* with the assistance of BCA Holdings in
Cape Breton.

Over the first year, various improvements were made in the Chac Lol
structure, especially with the formulation of roles. As part of the formation
program, two Mayan delegates were sent to Venezuela to participate in an
eco-tourism conference. IDRC helped fund this educational experience.
One campesino delegate happened to be the President of Chac Lol. Also,
two young Mayans came to Cape Breton to study English. They stayed
with local Mi'kmaqs in Eskasoni. None of the Mexicans involved in Yucape
speak English, so it was considered important to start an English learning
process. And what better place to learn English than Cape Breton?

Hotel. After much discussion with advisers in both the Yucatan and
Canada, we finally evolved a project which seemed to fit. By December of
1994 we had conceived of a Mayan Ecological Park which would include a
hotel. Eventually the local campesino association *(ejido)* turned over 30
acres of land to the project. The architectural students of the University of
Yucatan designed the development to include an arboretum, a botanical
garden, a restaurant, craft concessions and Mayan-style cabins for tourists. The site is actually only fifteen minutes from the famous Uxmal Pyramid, built in the year 600.

Botanical Garden and Arboretum. The transfer of technology was
significant on many fronts. Experts from the University of Chapingo developed vegetation plans for the botanical garden and the arboretum. The

botanical garden will contain the most important species from an economic point of view. This is logical since the Mayan people survived for a long time through their ability to harvest and use the natural vegetation without destroying the source.

Herbal Medicine. As well as classifying plants for commercial uses, such as dyes, and for cooking, the Chapingo experts are also planning a medicinal section. In that respect, the team is negotiating with the department of bio-chemistry at the University of Yucatan to assist in the classification and interpretation of traditional herbal medicines. The role of technology and science is fascinating here. The organizers do not have a romantic concept of quasi-magical herbal cures. They recognize a continuum between the traditional plant cures and the new pharmaceuticals developed in laboratories. Connected with this sub-project is a plan to establish an herbal medical clinic in an interior area where there is neither doctor nor hospital for over 10,000 square kilometers. Such a clinic could be an important experiment in alternative medicine.

Tourism. A Mayan owned tourist resort is especially significant in Mexico because most of the giant tourist centres are owned by the Japanese, the Spanish, or Americans. They are certainly not owned by the Mayans in the Yucatan. Instead, the Mayans are a kind of tourist attraction for the business interests. Worse, in the communities around the typical tourist sites, the Mayan language is not encouraged; indeed, it is discouraged. The trend is to preserve the Mayan buildings, but not the Mayan people and their culture. In contrast, the Chac Lol tourist project is in a Mayan speaking town and all employees must be able to speak Mayan. Besides being shown the physical ruins, the tourist will be treated to presentations by the living Mayans concerning their culture and traditions. Tourists will be invited to Mayan homes to meet their children and their animals.

At the time of writing, the Yucape project is still developing. As of 1997, it has not yet succeeded in developing a financial structure to support the hotel project. Nevertheless, it is worth including as a living example of an attempt to use some of the values found in the Mondragon and Valencia examples. It will certainly not look like Mondragon or Valencia. Nor will it resemble New Dawn. However, the working thesis of this book is that the essential element is not a particular structure or a quantity of assets. The essential is made up of certain principles and values that are transnational and transcultural. These values include a respect for technology while using it in a way that enhances a community. They concern a spirit of sharing so that the various economic units collaborate and act in an integrated manner for the good of the total community. It concerns a positive regard for people in the local community not only as a resource but as the ones who should control their own development.

In a project of this type, the key will be capital. The local wages, if one is lucky enough to have a job, are approximately five dollars per day. Hence it is difficult to set up a local community bank in the style of Mondragon or even something like BCA in Cape Breton. This could be a great opportunity for non-exploitative international investment. The architectural students are looking at local physical resources with enthusiasm and creativity. For instance, they would like to be able to use local stone for building projects, thus creating further spinoff jobs. For the foreign hotel-builders this would not even be a consideration, at least, as far as we have heard.

Throughout America there is a wide variety in the experimention going on in the area of community economic development. We have discussed a few and pointed out that there are many more which the reader should investigate. These experiments constitute a form of community learning. These projects have many differences but they all manifest a new spirit of community initiative and they all share some basic values that will make a constructive difference in our children's future.

Notes

1. Jack Quarter, *The Canadian Social Economy,* Toronto: Lorimer, 1992.
2. A more comprehensive treatment can be found in the recent book by Stewart Perry and Mike Lewis, *Re-inventing the Local Economy*, Vernon, B.C.: Centre for Community Enterprise, 1994.
3. Greg MacLeod, *New Age Business*, Ottawa: Canadian Council on Social Development, 1986.
4. The term "Community Development Corporation" has been commonly used in the USA. "Community Enterprise" is more common in the United Kingdom.
5. This data has been taken from reports by the West Coast Group of Annual Reports, Colville Investments.
6. The National Film Board of Canada has produced an excellent film about the Evangeline Group. It is entitled *We're the Boss.*
7. Data taken from the Annual Report of 1993.
8. "Class A shares, Seventh Edition" *Le Fonds de Solidarite des travailleurs de Quebec*, 1990, Montreal p. 3.
9. The reader may write to CCE Publicatons for a more complete list, see address in the appendix for *Making Waves Magazine.*
10. Report of the World Commission on Environment and Development, (Brundtland Commission) 1987, United Nations, New York.

11. It is interesting to note the parallel with GNP. David Simms was also a government employee who became involved with a local group and left the government to work full-time in the community.
12. Non-published Report of NGO Meeting of Nov. 1992 of the Canadian Embassy of Mexico City.

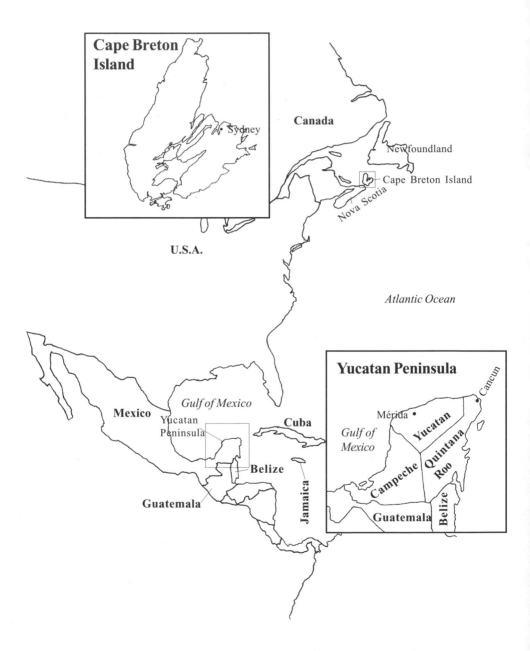

CHAPTER 8

PRACTICAL REFLECTIONS FOR COMMUNITY ECONOMIC SOLUTIONS

During the 1990's there has been a rising disillusionment with conventional corporate business. People have been shocked to learn of rising profits in major corporations, but yet rising layoffs of dedicated employees. This has prompted an increased interest in economic alternatives. Alternative business that is based on service to the community rather than simple profit is often referred to as the third sector, the voluntary business sector or the social economy. Claude Beland, head of the Desjardins credit union system in Quebec reacts to the term social economy:

"In a sense, the social economy is not new. It is the economy as it ought to be understood. The etymology tells us that "economy" signifies order in the household. It is evident that the economy ought to assure order and allow everyone to participate actively and with dignity in its development." (Speech by Claude Beland, *"Jeune Chambre de Commerce de Montreal"*, on "Good Corporate Citizenship," Dec. 5, 1996). He thus says that the economy today is not playing its proper role and that a reorientation of our business structures is urgently needed.

In the preceding chapters, the reader had the opportunity to see and judge concerning a variety of alternative forms of business. At this point, it is time to act. As J. Tompkins would say, it's time to put legs on these ideas.

NEW TECHNOLOGIES OF ORGANIZATION

In the twentieth century we have become accustomed to the thrill of announcements about new technological discoveries. Generally, we think of technology as being about machines. But we can also consider technology to be about the systematic processes of social economic organization. As Ursula Franklin pointed out in her Massey lectures of 1989, "Technology is a system. It entails far more than its individual material components. Technology involves organization, procedures, symbols, new words, equations, and, most of all, a mindset." [1] The huge international corporations are powerful, not only because of the machines they invent, but also because of the systems of resource organization they devise. Just as nuclear technology has often been used to harm rather than enhance communities, so also has social economic technology been used in such a way that it causes communities to decline and die rather than to grow and prosper. Mondragon and Valencia can be viewed as technological breakthroughs in how human-economic resources are organized for the benefit of the local society.

Nineteenth century thinkers saw well that whoever controls capital controls society. In the twentieth century we have seen that technology is just as important and perhaps more so for controlling the shape and style of society. Capital and technology, combined, create an extremely powerful force. The question is always whether such forces can be harnessed and submitted to ethical guidelines or whether they must be left free to follow the vagaries of the marketplace.

Mondragon and Valencia manifest a better and more hopeful way than capitalism for controlling and directing these great forces of technology and capital. In the sphere of mechanical and electronic technology, they compete with world-class corporations. In terms of "social technology" they are vastly superior. They have found a technique for capturing and orienting local capital for local development. They are examples of powerful corporate systems being intentionally directed to the good of local communities rather than to the profit of anonymous and distant shareholders. They are examples of a more holistic technology. Their guiding principle is that decisions should be based on what is best for their local communities. They contradict Friedman of the University of Chicago and many other professors of business who say that the only "rational" guide for business organization is private profit accumulation.

Communities all over America are suffering from the negative impact of our economic organizations from Chiapas in Mexico, through the slums of Los Angeles to the coal towns of Cape Breton. The new international economic order is not friendly to local community. In Mexico, campesinos leave their traditional homes and flock to pollution ridden Mexico City where the population is in excess of 22 million. Many thousands of jobless people sleep on the streets of New York. The unemployment levels in Newfoundland villages and in northern Manitoba exceed 25 per cent.

If the situation in the real world is offensive to us and if it contradicts our values, then we must change the world. In order to do so, we need capital and technological instruments. But what kind of technology? This is where Ursula Franklin's definition comes to bear. Technology is not just material but social and economic organization. It is generally admitted that we have a choice of values, but it has not been admitted that we have a choice in technology. It is our claim that we do have a choice of technology when it comes to the way we organize society and the economy. If the current technology of corporate organization and process is not appropriate to our value systems then we must invent new technologies of organization. Leaders in Mondragon and Valencia have done it in spite of what the business text-book writers say. It is important to distinguish between what the writers say and what business practitioners say. The refreshing experience of many people involved in community economic development is the discovery that there are business persons with communitarian values who would like to be able to modify and adapt their business practices to what they feel in their hearts. Most business persons do not like to see closed factories and long lines of people on unemployment and welfare.

If we view corporate business structures as a kind of technology, then we can say that the community groups described in the preceding chapter have been involved in technological experimentation. They want to solve the problems of unemployment, poverty and economic decline. The motives are clear. What is unclear is the nature of the technologies being developed and which of these works best. We could view the cooperative movements as earlier examples of holistic technology in the domain of business. During the last thirty years there has been an awareness that we need new kinds of organizational technology because the old cooperative structures are not adequate.

Just as some Spanish leaders in Mondragon and Valencia rejected the dogmas of the business schools as well as the dogmas of the old cooperative movement and sought new solutions, a significant number of people in America are also looking more and more to new corporate structures. In Mexico, university writers are now referring to the *empresa social* (social corporation). All over the United States economic community development groups are springing up.[2] In Canada there are a good number of experiments which indicate an ongoing search for new methods for the organization of our economic affairs. Although there is no case in the Americas that resembles the integrated models of Mondragon and Valencia, there is enormous potential. As Jack Quarter points out, there is a large unacknowl-edged body of economic entities that are neither government nor conventional private enterprise.[3]

These economic organizations, from cooperatives and community development corporations to day-care centers, constitute an untapped economic resource. He calls it a sleeping giant with tremendous unrecognized economic power.

The review of some examples of community oriented, alternative business initiatives in the last chapter makes it evident that none of them achieve the potential that could be reached if the Mondragon philosophy were adopted. It is not a case of duplicating Mondragon or Valencia; it is a case of adopting some of the basic values and techniques that could help make community business initiatives so much more effective. With a bit more thought and willingness to collaborate, these initiatives could become building blocks for the organization of powerful, community-based, comprehensive business corporations. They can be regarded as beginnings of a new movement that combines corporate business techniques with humanistic, community values.

A: COMMUNITY ECONOMIC DEVELOPMENT

While promoting this new alternative form of business corporation, I do not pretend that it can do the whole job required for community revitalization. No one organization can solve the problem because unemployment, social deterioration and poverty have deeper roots than business structures alone. Rather, community revitalization requires a dynamic strategy involving many kinds of organizations to address poverty and institutional decline. The general approach is often referred to as "Community Economic Development." Mike Lewis defines this term as:

> a comprehensive, multi-faceted strategy for the revitalization of community economies, with a special relevance to communities under economic and social stress. Through the development of organizations and institutions, resources and alliances are put in place that are democratically controlled by the community. They mobilize local resources (people, finances, technical expertise, and real property) in partnership with resources from outside the community for the purpose of empowering community members to create and manage new and expanded businesses, specialized institutions and organizations.[4]

A community based business, while only one element in this kind of broad approach to community development, is a fundamental and necessary one.[5] Any serious attack on poverty and decline requires all the resources listed. But although community based business is not the whole solution to the ills of society, it is a model that will help, and where there is poverty and unemployment our moral obligation is to use our imagination, including our new visions of business, in seeking solutions.

Instead of using the term community *development* corporation which suggests a very broad and comprehensive mission, I use the term "Community *Business* Corporation" (CBC) which implies a mission that is more narrow, but more likely to be achieved. The model is an attempt to appropriate some of the techniques of the conventional business corporations and adapt them to personalistic and community purposes. CBC is an enabling structure for carrying on business development over a spectrum of domains from the financial to the cultural. Though the ethos and goals are community improvement, the technique is similar to private business methods.

Since we are now entering the twenty-first century, it is high time that we broke away from our old mindsets which limit job initiatives as coming from "charities," "capitalistic enterprises" or "government agencies." The community business corporation is a model that breaks out of the old categories and has great potential for the future. This and other new kinds of business structures are rising as the old structures of communism crumble in the East. *The fatal economic mistakes of the communist system were the neglect of the free market and the failure to promote capital accumulation. The fatal error of modern capitalistic corporations has been the refusal to integrate ethical obligations and concerns for local welfare with powerful techniques of wealth creation.* As a general rule, both systems have reduced workers to mere numbers and cogs in a machine. Personal development was a non-issue in both industrial systems. The community business movement is fortunate in being able to avoid such errors and to take what is best from both systems.

Since the idea of a community business corporation assumes it will be owned and controlled by the people who live in the place where the corporation is located, its interests are not likely to oppose the local interest. The community business corporation is a tool that is especially appropriate for those communities which have been left out of current post-industrial developments. We may be looking at a part of the new model which will go further and even replace the present model of the national and international business corporation which operates independently of the commonly perceived public good in many domains.

143

B: GETTING STARTED

At this point we are making some assumptions about the reader. We assume that: 1) you are morally concerned about social economic justice, 2) that you are searching for solutions, and 3) that you want to contribute to a solution. Your contribution may be in the form of an investment in a community venture fund, or it may be in the form of an initiative to start a community business. Assuming a wide variety of readers, we have touched upon a wide variety of models from the urban, industrial case of Algoma, to the rural, depopulated regions where GNP and Kitsaki operate. This final section is intended to provide some orientation and guidelines for those who are thinking of action at some level.

The steps to the actual formation of a community business corporation are not especially complicated:

          1. Form a group
          2. Examine existing models
          3. Identify a business opportunity
          4. Organize a structure
          5. Seek out resources
          6. Launch into action

1. The Group

The group could be a self-appointed group of community activists as in Valencia or it could be delegates from a variety of community-minded organizations: fire department, labour union, board of trade, church group, credit union and so on. The first task of the group will be to discuss their opinions and intentions to ascertain that they share fundamental values.

In debates about development there is frequently confusion between structures and their underlying values. There is a basic difference that must be recognized. Structures, products and services may change, but for many of us, the underlying values must not change. It is possible that two commercial structures will be extremely different as far as size, products and organization are concerned, but underneath they could share the same values. On the other hand, it is possible to have two large industries which look the same in many respects, but whose underlying values are different. In the latter case a difference in values will usually come out when the time comes to distribute the profits.

Many of the pioneers of alternative structures found inspiration and values in their various religions and/or political movements, although they insisted that any worthwhile community business movement had to be non-sectarian in religion and politics. In spite of the differences, the values are strikingly similar. Most North American cooperative experiments which still survive, at least outside of Quebec, started during the depression of the 1920s and 1930s.

Unfortunately many people in the North American community and cooperative movements seem to think that the structural decisions of the 1920s and 1930s are sacred and must be maintained. Perhaps this is a problem of confusion between the ends and the means. I claim that the purpose or ends expressed by the Mondragon pioneers and those of the North American cooperative pioneers are the same. However, the instruments are different because the Mondragon system is open to changing structures and adapting to the world as it is. This principle of adaptation was expressed clearly at a meeting in Cheticamp, Cape Breton, in 1989.

A leader in the Quebec Desjardins movement stated that the group views credit unions as more than service agencies; they are instruments of economic development. He criticized many cooperatives who held to rhetorical values that didn't mean anything in practice. He explained that values are ideas to which we are committed by choice and which stimulate us to act in a particular way. Thus we can determine what people's values are by observing how they act in their daily lives. If it is not manifested somehow in concrete action then it is not a value.

The basic values in a variety of examples may be the same, but their order of importance and their formulation will change according to historical and cultural circumstances. For instance, in the eighteenth century, democracy was a priority in discussion of values. However, today it is taken for granted as a motherhood issue upon which everyone agrees. Thus in a certain sense it is not of great significance in producing a change in behaviour. The Desjardins delegate proposed solidarity with the local community as a more significant value in cooperativism today. This implies investment to promote more job-creating enterprises where unemployment exists.

It is extremely important for those involved in social-economic movements to ensure that they share the same ideas and vision through a process of discussion and updating of their ideas. If there are no shared significant ideas, then there will be no shared significant action.

2. Examine Models

As organizers try to develop a structure there is no point in trying to reinvent the wheel. They must devote time to a review of the existing cases to determine which are the best examples. This is a search for what is called "best practice." Action guided by a good dose of empiricism is healthier than simply acting from good intentions and second-hand ideas.

Deciding what is best practice calls for a large degree of objectivity but there is also a subjective element.

In trying to determine which community development businesses constitute the best practice or best models for us, it is worthwhile to develop a check-list. A check-list suggests that we have options, so before discussing what to choose, we should be very clear that some elements are not optional. Simply put, there are negotiables and non-negotiables in deciding what we expect of a community business corporation. The non-negotiables touch upon what we call "values." The over-riding value of all community business initiatives is the priority of the human and communal. All material resources, technology and capital must be subjugated clearly to the good of the local community, individually and collectively. This is not negotiable.

In looking at particular examples like Mondragon or New Dawn we will find that we are usually dealing with "more or less" rather than black and white. Nevertheless it is important to perform a critical analysis. What goes into a check-list will depend a great deal upon who we are, what our level of consciousness is and what our social history is. Therefore, each group should make their own list. I suggest that it be not "black and white" or "yes and no." For instance, Mondragon is strong on capital control but weak on gender equity. On the other hand, New Dawn is weak on capital control but strong on gender equity. New Dawn has medium insulation from the market but Mondragon has weak insulation from the market. Algoma and Vancity Credit Union are unifunctional and unisectoral while Valencia is multifunctional and multisectoral.

There is no limit to the kind and quantity of analysis that one could make of these various examples of community business. It can never be complete. The purpose of this text is to exemplify a method of critical thinking where the concrete structures and details are thought of in terms of values. Of course, there must be a limit. There must come a time when decisions are made. Otherwise the group ends up doing nothing: they become victims, according to the adage, of paralysis by analysis. An ethical stance means that we must act even though we are not too clear as to what is best.

When we can't quite make up our minds as to what is best we should visit other community enterprises; there is no replacement for face-to-face contact. An analogy could be made with the Mexican saying that seeing is the beginning of love. They do not find the practice of mail-order brides acceptable. Similarly, when we see a community business in operation and we talk to the people involved, then we can better judge what is good and what is bad about it, and what it is that we would like to do.

It is manifestly unethical to allow people to suffer through unemployment and poverty simply because we do not have all of the theory worked out. High ideals concerning a perfect community enterprise are never the justification for inaction.

3. Business Opportunities

Wherever there are three or four people gathered together, there exists a business opportunity. In Mondragon, they started making small stoves; in New Dawn, they bought an old building; in Mexico, they added value to the corn by processing; in Newfoundland, they added value to trees by processing them into flooring. Surprisingly, most people will discover business opportunities around them if they engage in brain-storming.

The group must ask two questions of a business opportunity. First, is it good for the local community, and secondly, will it make money. Money is always important in business. Some groups are reluctant to express a desire to "make money." Often they will simply prefer to "break even." Usually the groups who merely try to break even will go bankrupt. It is preferable to end up with surplus revenue or profit. The problem lies not in the making of profit. It concerns what we do with the profit. If we regard money as a means, and not an end, we will re-invest it to create more jobs for the unemployed. In seeking out an opportunity, it is wise to recruit a few successful business persons into the group. Business people are often flattered when community groups ask them to share their business intelligence.

4. Oganizational Structure

Having thus justified imperfection, I can propose a few organizational elements in a thought-out community business corporation that will differ from a conventional corporation: the role of the board, the question of employees and volunteers, and the importance of community enterprises collaborating with each other in a "zone" approach.

The Board. The board of a CBC is much more critical than that of a conventional corporation. It has a two-fold role:

(1)   to represent community concerns, and

(2)   to oversee the management of economic resources.

The first role is in contradistinction to the typical large corporation whose directors claim that they represent the interests of the shareholders. It is true that some cooperatives also say that their principal concern is the interest of the membership, even though the membership is a small minority, and sometimes predominantly middle-class. In a community business the board has to do what is best for the total community whether the total community is involved or not.

The second role concerns the ability to impose standards of efficiency. It implies the desire to find the manager who is able to perform with the greatest efficiency and productivity without contradicting social policy. It requires the courage to hire the most able person rather the one who is most loyal, "politically correct" and most connected with the board members.

Often the abilities to be socially conscious and "hard-nosed" do not coexist in the same person. The obvious technique is to seek a mixed board with different members representing different concerns and bringing different kinds of skills to the table.

One mistake many groups make is to allow political representatives to serve on their boards. It is often unfair to an elected politician to serve on a CBC board because it can happen that support of a decision that is good for the corporation will be bad for some of his or her constituents and thus cost an election. Also, the non-partisan nature of a CBC must be jealously protected. As Stewart Perry put it, after many years of experience in the United States: "In the field of Community Economic Development there are no permanent friends or enemies with regard to politicians."[6] Most organizers agree in strongly opposing any identification or alliance of a community business corporation with a partisan political group. Rather than represent particular individuals or particular partisan groups, this kind of corporation attempts to represent the good of the total community and, it is to be hoped, the values of the local community.

The Employees and Volunteers. The role of the employee in a CBC also changes by the fact that the intention is the achievement of community purposes and not simply the generation of profits. The employee now has to be more than a source of labour purchased by capital. The employee now becomes an associate in a common purpose. This nuances the ancient notion of a corporate person as "a group of individuals unified in a common purpose." In the distant past the common purpose could be a religious cult or it could be a secular, worldly pursuit such as organizing a group of associates to engage in commercial trade to raise money for the queen's treasury. Some commentators suggest that the medieval guilds were forerunners, in some respects, of the modern corporation.

The paradigm here, however, is the medieval monastery, which was certainly corporate. In this more traditional notion of a corporation, money is necessary but it is secondary.

When an employee is viewed as an associate, new forms and new structures for participation must be designed. Worker cooperatives are one form but there are others which range from group decision making to employee purchase of shares and profit sharing. Much more experimentation is required to discover the best methods for simultaneously fostering both personal input as well as operational efficiency. It is interesting that the nature of high technology processing also requires a much more collaborative and flexible attitude by workers.

It should be noted that this concept of the business corporation includes more than the salaried employee. The citizen volunteer is an essential associate and is not external to the basic operation. Association is established through activity and common intention, rather than by money. A typical community business such as New Dawn involves many local citizens as committee members. Their role is fundamental for the achievement of the New Dawn purpose.

The Manager. This book has attempted to avoid dogmatism in everything except the application of human values to the economy. A particularly difficult concept for progressive, community-based groups is the concept of "management." Especially in populist circles there is a dogmatic belief that everybody is capable of everything: that any member of the community could take on the role of manager. There is a reluctance to give management authority to one person over the others. Don José Maria was particularly strong in his criticism of this "false democratism." In commenting on the worker-owned cooperatives in France, he attributed their frequent failure to a tendency to rely on "consensus management" rather than to trust the competence and authority of one manager. Many traditional writers have said that labour and capital are the factors of production. Don José Maria adds a third, "the manager." [7]

This insight concerning management is connected with the development of technology during this century. Many kinds of industries require sophisticated technologies which are not easily understood. If we wish to use improved technology in a community business, we are going to have to admit that we require managers with special competence and we are going to have to give them authority. It is quite strange that community groups readily admit that a carpenter has skills that the group does not possess and will allow the carpenter to make decisions concerning the construction of a building, but when it comes to admitting that business managers have special skills and knowledge, they resist.

In the Mondragon system, political control remains with the workers. The workers and their board appoint the manager, and they can dismiss the manager. However, once the manager is appointed, the manager is the boss. In very small, family-like enterprises, this kind of authority is obviously not necessary. However, as an enterprise becomes larger and more sophisticated, strong management becomes more necessary.

In arguing that authority has to be delegated to and reside mainly in one person, even in a workers' cooperative, we are not ignoring all the advances in modern management where participation and consultation is the order of the day. Mondragon is very strong on management committees and channels of open communication, but no manager can escape accountability and responsibility by saying that a committee "made me do it." A distinction that many organizers fail to make is between the political control of the corporation and control of the day to day management. It is possible to be very democratic in the social and political orientation of the business and yet to delegate management control to one person. If the manager does not perform adequately, then the board can dismiss that person.

It is extremely difficult to find good managers for community businesses. The reason is that such managers require all the skills of a conventional manager plus social skills and moral commitment. Many conventional business managers have as their only objective the making of profit. In contrast, the manager of a community business must not only make money, but assure that the social and community objectives of the corporation are met. In this book, great emphasis has been put on the necessity of accessing technology and capital. However, the necessary resource that is most difficult to find is management.

5. Seek Resources

No business can function without resources. The Mondragon Triangle is a good summary of resources needed: technology, finance and formation. An often neglected source of both technology and formation for community groups is the educational system: schools, colleges and universities. Since these institutions are paid for out of tax dollars, they can be expected to provide service to the local community. Many professors and teachers are happy to be invited to work with community groups as an opportunity to test their ideas in practice.

Government agencies also should be regarded as resources available to community groups. In the case of BCA, it was considered that Enterprise Cape Breton Corporation could be a supporting partner in providing a loan to match local funds raised. In Canada and in other developed countries there are a wide variety of tax credits and incentive grants to promote local development. It is important for the local community group to ask government agencies what resources they are able to provide.

Finance is always difficult but we have seen examples in Chapter 7 where a number of groups started with borrowed money. However, finance, as well as other needed resources, especially the human resource of management, is often available if the group is willing to enter into alliances with similar groups in the same geographic zone.

The Zone Consortium. Michael Porter has become the guru of modern business in promoting the notion of related business clusters.[8] From a purely business point of view it often makes sense for business to act as a related group, and to share services, technology, and capital. Actually Mondragon and Valencia are superb examples of commercial clustering. Verdu, the authority on Valencia quotes A. Antoni who insists on interlinkages between community businesses in the same geographic zone:

> Isolated, worker owned businesses merit sympathy, justify curiosity, but cannot pretend to exercise any social or economic influence. It is only as federated in the bosom of like-minded businesses that well designed businesses such as worker cooperatives can obtain decisive support and significant expansion.[9]

Professor Michael Piore of MIT also stresses the importance of businesses collaborating in groups. He takes the example of Emilia Romagna in Italy, north of Rome. Here there are many cases of worker ownership and commercial collaboration amongst businesses. Business professors such as Piore refer to this kind of collaboration as examples of "regulation theory." It is a means of regulating output from one geographic zone through organizing a number of business firms into an integrated constellation. Instead of businesses in one small geographic zone competing with one another, they collaborate. The result is that competition between zones develops.[10]

Although cooperatives and credit unions tend not to operate as consortia in America because of the American accent on individualism and autonomy, the International Cooperative Alliance lists "cooperation among cooperatives" as a guiding principle. Most community development corporations and various forms of community business also tend to act as autonomous units, each proud of their individual achievements. Because of this they miss out on so many opportunities that would permit them to grow and expand so as to become more effective in fighting unemployment and poverty.

The great lesson of Mondragon and Valencia, and also the lesson of the capitalistic business world, is that it makes sense both commercially and socially to collaborate. When a variety of community oriented businesses in one local community are suffering economic distress, then there is a social obligation to pool resources for the common good. Isolationism has been a tremendous disadvantage for many traditional community groups.

The formula for success as demonstrated in Mondragon is to form a consortium which shares not only the same community vision but which also shares the same commercial resources. The key elements of such a consortium must be:

1. a financial business which provides financing,
2. businesses which sell products and/or services,
3. research centres which keep the consortium up to date (usually found in the university or college),
4. an educational institution which provides formation.

Atlantic Co-op in Atlantic Canada proposed this strategy a number of years ago but the local leaders really did not see the point.[11] It has taken a long time for the community business sector to realize that this kind of clustering and joint-venturing is useful and even necessary for community businesses that wish to grow. As we promote the zone or division approach, we should also bear in mind the kind of balance suggested by Jesus Larranaga, one of the Mondragon founders: "While federating, we must maintain the maximum level of local autonomy that is compatibile with economies of scale and strategic planning for the group."[12] Often groups federate on a regional or a national level, and neglect to federate at the level of county, town or city. Mondragon teaches us that groups are more effective when they first unite in their immediate area. The local federation can then federate at the regional level. Traditionally this is called the "Principle of Subsidiarity."

6. Launch into Action

In a world that is increasingly complex and overpowering, many of us feel powerless. We hear repeatedly, "Nothing can be done. The problems are too big for us." The message of this whole book is that we can do something and indeed we must do something. It is much better to have tried and failed than not to have tried at all. At least we will have preserved our humanity. Therefore, readers are urged simply to launch into action.

C: PERSON-CENTERED ECONOMICS

In spite of all I have said about technology, finance and research, the success of every major, successful community business seems to depend on the leadership of some outstanding person who worked with a small group of five or six persons.

Most successful programs arise out of local initiatives, rather than top-down strategies, and develop through independent, usually non-profit entities. They are led by "social entrepreneurs," most often local leaders who combine social vision, organizing skill and political acumen with the tenacity and business management skills needed to perform in this very difficult arena, and through very difficult times. These professionals, whom we refer to as development managers, are in short supply. [13]

In the case of Mondragon we had Don José Maria; in Valencia, Josep Soriano; in the Solidarity Fund of Quebec, Louis Laberge; in Evangeline, Leonce Bernard; in GNP, David Simms; in HRD, Harold Crowell; in SIMA-Caraquet, Raymond Gionet and Gilles Menard; in Colville, Don MacMillan, and the list goes on. It seems that there is always need for a person who is willing to sacrifice and commit time and energy. Often it means sacrificing financial rewards. However, it is never the case of a lone cowboy operating alone. It is always a person working closely with a small team of equally committed persons. Then there are the various volunteers who serve on committees. There are also the fulltime employees who are not just employees, but fully committed as persons. When all is said and done the most important element which makes this kind of corporation successful is the human element. It is people in a corporate organization working efficiently with the best of technology to make life better for themselves and other people in their own community.

The point of this book has been to seek a new and better business model for community groups wishing to take more control over their local economy and to direct it to the creation of jobs and the improvement of working life. I chose Mondragon as a working model. When I looked at many other cases, I realized that the underlying values are the most important element. The products and structures will differ, but if the underlying values are there, we will make our communities better places to live in, not only for a fortunate elite but for all who wish to participate. While giving credit to the old cooperative movement and to the new kinds of community economic initiatives mentioned above, I recognize that we still have a long way to go in evolving effective new models for a changed economy.

The social-economic problems that face us are enormous. Yet we must do something if we are to call ourselves human. A few years ago the problem of political change in South Africa was seen as insurmountable. A journalist asked Bishop Desmond Tutu how it was possible to keep going on in the face of such immense problems and obstacles. His counter question was, "How do you eat an elephant?" Tutu answered the question for the puzzled journalist: "One bite at a time."

In the same vein, a group of Latin American social activists held a series of study-sessions in Brazil with some of the best intellectuals in the region. Having analyzed all of the problems concerning the multinational corporations, the immense debts in their various countries, the problems of illiteracy, disease, starvation and corruption, they concluded that there was no really rational ground for believing that any reform group could succeed in changing the system. Their final conclusion was that trust in rational arguments could not be the basis for action. Rather, they proposed hope and faith in their neighbours as the basis for action. So they advised everyone to go back home as bearers of hope and to do what they could in their own local communities.

To have hope like this, which is necessary for action, may seem foolish in a rational view of the immense power of the international corporate structure. However, perhaps this is the only way to be human in a sometimes inhuman society.

With a good dose of faith in each other, and armed with the examples illustrated in the preceding chapters, we can begin to form a new model for community business that is person centered. In this age of giant business and giant government, where small community groups feel powerless against forces which are destructive of their fundamental values, the community business approach offers an appropriate technology that is within the reach of all of us. It is something doable for those who are concerned about unemployment and the decline of our communities. It is something that we can do which is based upon traditional values of sharing and mutual responsibility. It is old-fashioned in many ways, but if we are to have a future, it is also the way of the future.

Notes

1. *The Real World of Technology*, Massey Lectures, CBC Enterprises, Toronto, 1990, p.12.
2. Cf. Stewart Perry, *Communities on the Way,* Albany: SUNY Press, 1987.
3. Jack Quarter, *Canada's Social Economy*, Toronto: Lorimer, 1992.
4. Mike Lewis, paper delivered at the International Institute for Sustainable Development, Winnipeg, June, 1994.
5. In his book *Communities on the Way*, Stewart Perry gives a very comprehensive analysis of the complexity of the problem.
6. Cf. Stewart Perry, *Communities on the Way,* Albany: SUNY Press, 1987.
7. Cf, ch. 4, section D.
8. Porter, Michael, "Competitive Advantage," New York, Free Press, 1985.
9. Verdu, *op. cit.* p. 148

10. Piore, M.J. and Sabel, C.F., "Second Industrial Divide: Possibilities for Prosperity," 1984, Basic Books, New York.
11. Stewart Perry and Mike Lewis, *Re-inventing the Local Economy,* Vernon, B.C., Centre for Community Enterprise, 1994.
12. Jesus Larranaga, *Don José Maria y la Experiencia Cooperativa de Mondragon*, Mondragon: Caja Laboral, 1981, p. 171.
13. Mike Lewis, *op. cit,* sect. 84.

POSTSCRIPT: THE DEBATE

Like so many founders of social-economic movements, if they could see how their project evolved, Don José Maria would be surprised and puzzled by the giant international Mondragon Cooperative Corporation of today. By 1997 Mondragon had established subsidiary factories in Argentina, England and China. These resemble subsidiaries of General Electric or any other large multinational corporation. Also in Spain, the cooperative retail systems of Eroski of Mondragon and Consum of Valencia have joined forces to create a holding company called Erosmer.

Erosmer is now setting up subsidiary supermarkets throughout Spain as private stock companies. The Eroski group owns 51% of the shares with the other shares being owned by venture capital groups such as ONCE, a managed fund owned by the national organization for the blind in Spain.

The reality of the retail food business is that small companies do not survive well. The Eroski group is now one of the giants. It is number three in Spain. The two top grocery chains are multinationals. Number four is another multinational. If Eroski did not go big there would be very little Spanish control in the food business. However, it should be noted that, even if the Eroski chain looks like the multinationals, there are important differences.

Among the differences, one concerns the fact that, within the Mondragon and Valencia areas the retail stores are still cooperatively run. Both Eroski and Consum have central elected boards. Each of the two central boards has 12 members: six employees and six consumers. The consumers are usually delegates from other cooperatives. While each local consumer store does not have a management board, it does have a consumer quality-control committee. The consumer committee provides continual input into management concerning quality of products and services. The multinationals do not do this. Another difference involves the promotion of locally produced products, especially products from its own community-owned producer systems. On the shelves of Eroski stores one will find a surprisingly high percentage of Eroski produced goods. A further difference is the policy of selling 8% of the shares to the supervisory staff of each non-cooperative Eroski supermarket.

The debate about the seeming contradiction in philosophy is deeply rooted. It is similar to the debate among the personalist philosophers in the early part of this century. Some said that cooperative, democratic businesses could not survive in a capitalistic dog-eat-dog society. Others said that it is possible to organize democratic, socially responsible businesses in a hostile competitive economy. Don José Maria took the optimistic side, hoping that new democratic businesses would influence the others. Leaders in Mondragon and Valencia say that they hold to their original philosophy of promoting participation and serving the larger community but they recognize the hard, cold realities of the international economy. If they had not expanded the Eroski cooperative store system to the whole of Spain then they would have been swamped by the multinational grocery chains that have lower prices through economies of scale. They judged it impossible to maintain a small chain of worker and community owned stores and still remain competitive in price and product range. The only option they saw was to go big or disappear altogether. To organize worker-owned supermarkets in other cities like Madrid and Grenada was simply not practical. With multinationals analyzing every city for market penetration, decisions had to be made rapidly and these decisions involved many complex factors, such as sophisticated technology, which are beyond ordinary citizens and ordinary workers. So, the end result is that a cooperative, community-owned complex is flourishing in Mondragon but its health and even survival depends to some extent on its non-cooperative subsidiaries in other centres and in other countries.

There is a parallel situation in the area of electro-domestic products and automobile parts. Huge multinationals have the dominant control. Over 30% of Mondragon production is exported. If the original factories in Mondragon stay as they are they will be put out of business by the competition; they simply will not last if they rely on the local market. Yet they cannot organize democratic factories in England or the United States. So they simply buy subsidiaries, sometimes in strategic partnerships with other corporations. Also, they will accept contracts to produce components for large capitalist corporations like General Electric.

Mondragon leaders face a very real dilemma. If they stick to their original worker-owner system, then harm will be done in that workers in Mondragon will eventually lose their jobs. If they participate in the capitalist, multinational system then they will go against their original democratic philosophy. I think that Don José Maria Arrizmendiarrieta would have seen this as a classical problem of life. In such a dilemma, where one is faced with an evil on both sides, the rule is to choose the lesser of two evils. This, the leaders of Mondragon have done, but they have done it reluctantly. They did it not because they wanted to, but because they were forced to, and that is a good ethical stance.

The trend towards mergers and giant conglomerates became very clear during the 1990s. For example, in May of 1997, the Grand Metropolitan Corporation and Guinness Corporation announced what soon became known in London as the blockbuster merger of the year. It involved combining under one corporate umbrella such diverse companies as Haagen Daaz ice cream, Bell Whiskey, Burger King, Johnny Walker Whiskey and Guinness Stout. This new corporate combination was valued at over 50 billion dollars. Part of the rationale was that 2,000 jobs could be cut from the combined workforce of 85,000.(The Times of London, p. 31, May 13, 1997.)

This last fact brings out a fascinating basic difference between the traditional corporation and the Mondragon Corporation. In its five-year strategic plan for 1997-2002 MCC projected the creation of 8,800 new jobs. While the traditional capitalist corporations merge to reduce jobs, the community-oriented Mondragon Corporation merges to create jobs. This manifests a very fundamental difference in the underlying philosophies. Professional management and efficiency can be instruments to impoverish communities or they can be instruments to enrich communities. The difference lies in the vision and the philosophy.

The debate in Mondragon concerning the tension between efficiency and participation is not unique. The same kind of dilemma exists in Eficoop in Mexico, in New Dawn/BCA in Canada and in most cases where community-based groups organize business enterprises. There seems to be an inherent tension or even a contradiction between efficient wealth creation and democratic participation. Professional management is necessary for efficiency and wealth creation, but professional management can only function with authority delegation and indirect democracy. It has often happened that cooperative, community businesses destroyed themselves in resisting outside control and insisting on local decision making. The worthy goal of local democratic control led to incompetent people attempting to make decisions in highly technical matters that they simply did not understand. It is not a question of being malicious or self-seeking, it is simply a fact of life that most businesses in our technological age require systems and networks with highly trained, sophisticated managers. This kind of debate is an ongoing one. It is paralleled in our general political system. The ideal kind of political system would be one of continual referendums where every citizen had an equal say in all decisions. Thomas More in his Utopia of the 16th century designed a marvelous democratic system, but it depended upon all citizens becoming well educated and morally enlightened. No one has been able to implement such an ideal system up to now. Most countries have chosen a system of representative democracy with a great number of indirectly delegated powers. The system works more or less for most people, but is certainly not satisfactory for the poor and the unemployed.

For some activists in the cooperative movement the essence of cooperatives is participation. Some cooperatives refuse to participate in larger networks and ventures through fear of losing control. They would rather remain small and democratic than grow bigger and have to submit to limits imposed from beyond their local neighbourhood. A good number of cooperatives are commercially successful following this strong localized formula. They have their autonomy. However, some could consider this a selfish view. It can happen that such a cooperative is providing wealth and security for its five hundred or so members but that outside that cooperative there are masses of poor and unemployed. Perhaps Kropotkin was thinking of this when he signaled the danger of cooperatives becoming exercises in collective egoism. The Mondragon leaders would say that each cooperative has a duty to expand and create jobs as long as there are unemployed people in the community. If a cooperative is profitable, it has all the more obligation to set aside part of its profits and to invest in the development of new businesses. Likely, the International Cooperative Alliance was thinking this way when it added as one of the basic principles of the cooperative movement: "Cooperatives work for the sustainable development of their communities through policies approved by their members."

In this book we have looked at Mondragon and Valencia in Spain, and a number of smaller examples of Canadian community initiatives to set up businesses dedicated to the common good. The ones that survive seem to be the ones that maintain a set of ideals and values but who admit that these cannot be all achieved. Rather, they hold the ideals as a kind of horizon at which they aim. Progress is judged not simply in attaining the ideal, but rather on coming close to the ideal. Of course there is the danger in that the incomplete, compromise situation will be accepted as the ideal and that no effort will be made to change and improve what we have. Open debate and free criticism helps to prevent this. If we follow the TU Lankide magazine, we see that this debate does go on in Mondragon.

While almost every other corporation in the world is cutting back and reducing the number of employees, MCC has as part of its five-year plan the goal of creating at least 8,800 new jobs in Spain. This is accepted as a duty to the general community which is suffering from unacceptably high levels of unemployment. While, for the Guinness Corporation, the priority is to increase profits, the priority for Mondragon is to increase jobs and preserve the community. This manifests the over-riding fidelity of Mondragon to its most basic distinguishing characteristic: The Priority of People Over Capital.

APPENDIX I

Biographical Sketch of Don José Maria Arrizmendiarrieta

Don José Maria was born in the town of Markina, in the Basque province of Vixcaya in Northern Spain, at one p.m. on April 22, 1915 (Taurus). He died in Mondragon at 8:20 on the evening of November 29, 1976 at the age of 61.

1928 - at the age of 12 years, he entered the college of Castilo-Elexabeita to study humanities and philosophy. He continued on to study theology in the seminary.

1936 - Franco led the fascist rebellion against the Spanish Republic.

1937 - José Maria left the seminary to join the Basque Army. He was then 21 years of age. He had not completed his Theological Studies. He was appointed journalist for the Basque Military News Service.

1939 - Franco defeated the forces of the Republic and Don José Maria was taken prisoner by the victorious Fascists. He was listed for execution but through a fortuitous error, he was passed over and survived. Upon release, he resumed his studies under a private tutor.

1940, 21 December - He was ordained priest by the Bishop of Vitoria which city is near Mondragon. At his own request he was scheduled to study Sociology at the University of Louvain in Belgium. He had been a disciple of French personalists such as Maritain and Mounier. This plan was canceled by church authorities.

1941, February - Don José Maria was named to the parish of Mondragon where he remained till his death.

Don José Maria's Ministry

Three Phases:

I. Early Years - 1941 to 1956

Don José Maria engaged in typical pastoral work. Much of his time was spent in the formation of youth such as the Young Christian Worker movement. During this period he set up the technical-trade school for youth.

II. Work or Job-Creation - 1956 to 1973

Don José Maria openly supported the idea of a new reformed economy. At a clergy meeting, in answer to criticism of his "worldliness," he said; "If the gospel does not apply to the economy, then to what does it apply?" He referred to the Church as a sign of contradiction.

Don José Maria assisted the team of five former students of the technical school to set up their worker-owned businesses. During this period he acted as supporter, mentor and stimulator of new business endeavours.

III. Quality of Life Issues - 1973 to 1976

Don José Maria reflected and spoke on the deeper problems of society, wondering how to personalize or humanize the economy. The disappearance of the concept of leisure concerned him as well as the problem of retired people in society.

APPENDIX II

B List Of Mondragon Enterprises (109)

(6 Enterprises)

ARO LEASING
C/ Gran Via, 35-6
48009 Bilbao
(Bizkaia)
Tel: (4) 416 82 66
Fax: (4) 416 67 62
ACTIVITIES:
Leasing, capital
goods

CAJA LABORAL
CREDIT
COOPERATIVE
P. José M.
Arrizmendiarrieta, s/n.
20500 Mondragon
(Guipuzcoa)
Tel: (43) 79 01 00
Fax: (43) 79 88 76
ACTIVITIES:
Banking

**LAGUN-ARO
VOLUNTARY
SOCIAL
WELFARE ENTITY**
P. José M.
Arrizmendiarrieta,
s/n.
20500 Mondragon
(Guipuzcoa)
Tel: (43) 79 01 00
Fax: (43) 79 64 44
ACTIVITIES:
Social welfare
cover for
cooperators

**LAGUN-ARO
VIDA**
(Shareholding)
C/Gran Via, 35-1

48009 Bilbao
(Bizkaia)
Tel: (4) 416 01 00
Fax: (4) 416 98 03
ACTIVITIES:
Life insurance

LAINTER
José M.
Arrizmendiarrieta,
n.5
20500 Mondragon
(Guipuzcoa)
Tel: (43) 79 01 00
Fax: (43) 79 64 44
ACTIVITIES:
Shopping centre
promotion

**SEGUROS
LAGUN-ARO**
(Shareholding)
C/Gran Via, 35-1
48009 Bilbao
(Bizkaia)
Tel: (4) 416 01 00
Fax: (4) 416 98 03
ACTIVITIES:
General insurance

(80 Enterprises)

**A. MACHINE
TOOL DIVISION
(12)**

**DANOBAT
SORALUCE**
Apraiz Kalea, 1
20870 Elgoibar
Guipuzcoa
tel: 43) 74 36 00

fax: 43) 74 37 67
Acitivities:
Project
engineering and
fabrication of
specialty machine
tools

DANOBAT
Arriago Kalea, 21
Apdo. 28
20870 Elgoibar
(Guipuzcoa)
Tel: (43) 74 02 50
Fax: (43) 74 31 38
ACTIVITIES:
Machinse -CNC:
cylinders,lathes,
automatic center
lathes, gantry type
machines, robots.

**ESTARTA
RECTIFICADORA**
c/Autonomia, 1
Apdo. 80
20870 Elgoibar
Tel: 43) 74 37 05
Fax. 43) 74 17 58
Activities:
Manufacture of
Electrical
Alternators

GOITI
Pol. Ind. Arriaga
Apdo. 80
20870 Elgoibar
Tel: 43) 74 03 50
Fax: 43) 74 30 86
Activities: Laser-
cutting machines

LEALDE
Apdo. 11
48280 Lekeitio
(Vizcaya)

Tel: (4) 684 01 51
Fax: (4) 684 27 61
ACTIVITIES:
Horizontal and
vertical CNC
lathes.

SORALUCE
B. Osintxu
20570 Bergara
(Guipuzcoa)
Tel: (43) 76 45 40
76 24 46
Fax: (43) 76 51 28
ACTIVITIES:
Moving column
milling machines,
transfer
machinery and
flexible
systems,radial
drills.

DOIKI
Pol. Ind, Goitondo, 5
48269 Mallabia
(Vizcaya)
Tel: (43) 17 16 00
Fax: (43) 17 42 73
ACTIVITIES:
Dimensional
tooling. High
precision
mechanics.
Electronic,
pneumatic and
mechanical
gauges. Machining
fixtures.

EGURKO
Basusta Bidea, n. 9
Apdo. 25
20750 Zumaia
(Guipuzcoa)
Tel: (43) 86 01 00
Fax: (43) 14 31 07

ACTIVITIES:
Edge banding
machines.
Shapers.
Combined
machines (edger
and shapers.)
Sanders.

KENDU
Pol. Industrial, s/n
20214 Segura
(Guipuzcoa)
Tel: (43) 80 13 40
Fax: (43) 80 19 05
ACTIVITIES:
High speed steel
cutters. Hard metal
cutters.

LATZ
Avda. de los
Gudaris, s/n
Apdo. 56
20140 Andoain
(Guipuzcoa)
Tel: (43) 59 25 07
Fax: (43) 80 19 05
ACTIVITIES:
Standard HSS and
HSSCO drill bits.
Hard metal drill bits.

ORTZA
Pol. Areta, s/n
31620 Huarte -
Pamplona
(Navarra)
Tel: (48) 33 04 38
Fax: (48) 33 00 02
ACTIVITIES:
Square-cut and
cross-cut saws

ZUBIOLA
B. Landeta, s/n
20730 Azpeitia
(Guipuzcoa)
Tel: (43) 81 40 00
Fax: (43) 81 40 08
ACTIVITIES:
HSS drill bits. MD
drill bits. HSS
cutters. MD
cutters. Saw
blades.

Cutterheads.
Window units.
Cutters.

**B. ENGINEERING
DIVISION (11)**

BERRIOLA
B. San Esteban s/n
20170 Usurbil
(Guipuzcoa)
Tel: (43) 36 60 90
Fax: (43) 37 00 94
ACTIVITIES:
DC motors.
Permanent magnet
servomotors.
Thyristor
regulators,
transistor
regulators.
Asynchronous
drives. Vectorial
frequency
converters.
Brushless drives.
Repair of motors
and regulators.

**FAGOR
AUTOMATION**
B. San Andrés, s/n
Apdo. 144
20500 Mondragon
(Guipuzcoa)
Tel: (43) 79 95 11
Fax: (43) 79 17 12
ACTIVITIES:
Numerical and
control systems.
Digital readouts.
Linear and rotary
transducers. Feed
and headstock
regulators. Feed
and headstock
motors.

DIARA
Pol. Basabe
Edif. Oficinas
EO13-14
20550
Aretzabaleta
(Guipuzcoa)
Tel: (43) 77 10 15

Fax: (43) 79 05 87
ACTIVITIES:
Product design.
Packaging design.
Graphic design;
corporate image.
Product
development.
Consulting and
design
management.
Interior design.

**LKS
CONSULTORIA**
P. José M.
Arrizmendiarieta
Edificio LK-3
20500 Mondragon
(Guipuzcoa)
Tel: (43) 77 03 35
Fax: (43) 77 10 12
ACTIVITIES:
Consulting(Strategic
planning,
marketing, legal
counsel,
engineering
consulting, qulaity
control etc)

LKS INGENIERIA
P. José M.
Arrizmendiarieta
Edificio LK-3
20500 Mondragon
(Guipuzcoa)
Tel: (43) 77 03 35
Fax: (43) 77 10 12
ACTIVITIES:
Engineering
consulting,
appraisals, civil
engineering,
quality-control etc.

ONDOAN
Parque
Tecnologico
Edificio 101 -
Modulo C
48016 Zamudio
(Vizcaya)
Tel: (4) 452 23 13
Fax: (4) 452 10 47
ACTIVITIES:

Sewage treatment
and water
purification. Fire
protection. Air
conditioning and
energy saving.
Environmental
engineering. Risk
analysis.
Hydrometallurgy.

**FAGOR
ARRASATE**
B. San Andrés
Apdo. 18
20500 Mondragon
(Guipuzcoa)
Tel: (43) 79 20 11
Fax: (43) 79 96 77
ACTIVITIES:
Sheet metal
products,
Stamping systems,
Processing
systems. Presses.
Die-making. After
sales service.

**FAGOR
SISTEMAS**
Apdo. 198
20500
Aretzabaleta
(Guipuzcoa)
Tel: (43) 77 11 93
Fax: (43) 77 00 66
ACTIVITIES:
Automated
manufacturing
systems

AURRENAK
Vitorialanda, 15
(Ali-Gobeo)
01010 Vitoria
(Alva)
Tel: (45) 24 48 50
Fax: (45) 24 69 12
ACTIVITIES:
Casting moulds
and patterns.
Tooling for
vulcanizing
industry.

Appendix II

ONO-PRES
B. de Ugarte, s/n
48510 Valle
Trapaga
(Vizcaya)
Tel: (4) 499 27 00
Fax: (4) 499 92 28
ACTIVITIES:
Hydraulic presses.

**BATZ
TROQUELERIA**
B. Torrea, 32-34
48140 Igorre
(Vizcaya)
Tel: (4) 631 57 07
Fax: (4) 631 55 66
ACTIVITIES:
Dies. Automations
systems. Jacks.
Pedals. Hand
brake levers.

**C.
AUTOMOTIVE
COMPONENTS
(8)**

BATZ SISTEMAS
B. Torrea, 32-34
48140 Igorre
(Vizcaya)
Tel: (4) 631 57 07
Fax: (4) 631 55 66
ACTIVITIES:
Automobile Parts.

FAGOR EDERLAN
B. Landeta
20540 Eskoriatza
(Guipuzcoa)
Tel: (43) 71 42 00
Fax: (43) 71 42 42
ACTIVITIES:
Suspension arms.
Knuckles.
Flywheels and
pulleys.
Mechanism
casings. Oil and
water pumps.
Clutch housings.
Gear box covers.
Discs-Drums.
Manifolds.
Paupers.

LUZURIAGA, V.
C/ Txiki-Erdi
20170 Usurbil
(Guipuzcoa)
Tel: (43) 37 02 00
Fax: (43) 36 55 64
ACTIVITIES:
Engine blocks and
cylinder heads.
Nodular casting.

MAPSA
(IRTAL, s. Coop)
Ctra. Echauri, 11
31160 Orcoyen
(Navarra)
Tel: (48) 32 50 11
Fax: (48) 32 52 23
ACTIVITIES:
Manufacture of
aluminum hubs.
Water pumps and
housings.
Aluminum parts
cast in low
pressure and
gravity moulds.

CIKAUTXO
B. Magdalena, 2, B
48710 Beriatua
(Vizcaya)
Tel: (4) 613 90 00
Fax: (4) 613 91 75
ACTIVITIES:
Technical rubber
parts for
automotive and
domestic
appliance sectors.
Rubber mixtures.

**FPK (50%
shareholding)**
B. San Antolin, 16
48010 Zamudio
(Vizcaya)
Tel: (4) 452 11 64
Fax: (4) 452 12 10
ACTIVITIES:
GMT plastic parts

MAIER
Pol. Ind. Arabieta,
s/n
Apdo. 103

48300 Gernika
(Vizcaya)
Tel: (4) 625 14 50
Fax: (4) 625 13 04
ACTIVITIES:
Plastic injection
moulding. Die
making. Finishes:
chrome plating,
screen printing,
stamping, painting,
laser, etc.

MATRIPLAST
B. San Antolin, 16
48010 Zamudio
(Vizcaya)
Tel: (4) 452 11 64
Fax: (4) 452 12 10
ACTIVITIES:
SMC plastic parts.

**D. DOMESTIC
APPLIANCE AND
ELECTRONIC
COMPONENTS
(7)**

COPRECI
Avada.de Alava, 3
20550
Artetxabaleta
(Guipuzcoa)
Tel: (43) 79 45 00
Fax: (43) 79 23 49
ACTIVITIES:
Gas components
(Stoves).
Electromechanical
components
(washing
machines).
Microwave
components
(ovens).

EIKA
Apdo. 20
48270 Markina
(Vizcaya)
Tel: (4) 616 77 32
Fax: (4) 616 77 44
ACTIVITIES:
Electric hobs.
Electric heating
elements.
Vitroceramic hobs.

EMBEGA
Pol. Industrial, s/n
Apdo. 63
31200 Estella
(Navarra)
Tel: (48) 54 13 53
Fax: (48) 54 13 62
ACTIVITIES:
Trims: screen
printed aluminium,
anodized
aluminium, painted
iron. Elastomer
seals. Membrane
keyboards.

**FAGOR
ELECTRONICA**
B. San Andrés, s/n
Apdo. 33
20500 Mondragon
(Guipuzcoa)
Tel: (43) 79 10 11
Fax: (43) 79 68 47
ACTIVITIES:
Seminconductors:
power diodes,
Zener diodes and
transient
suppressor
diodes. Radio
frequency
components: TV
tuners. TV signal
reception
components:
Satellite (SMATV)
MATV
Teledistribution.
Design of Radio
Frequency
equipment.

MATZ-ERREKA
Apdo. 86
20570 Bergara
(Guipuzcoa)
Tel: (43) 76 60 00
Fax: (43) 76 63 75
ACTIVITIES:
Nuts and bolts and
hot stamped parts.
Transformation of
plastic by injection.
Mould
construction. Door

and shutter raising systems.

ORKLI
Ctra. Zaldibia
20240 Ordizia
(Guipuzcoa)
Tel: (43) 88 07 00
Fax: (43) 88 73 08
ACTIVITIES:
Manual radiator valves and thermostates. Ball valves. Safety valves and units. Motor-driven valves. Thermoelectrical safety devices. Magnetic units. Thermocouples.

TAJO
Zona Ind.
Aranguren
B. Arragua
20180 Oiartzun
(Guipuzcoa)
Tel: (43) 49 03 75
Fax: (43) 49 13 63
ACTIVITIES:
Plastic processing and decoration. Mould construction for plastic injection.

E. INDUSTRIAL COMPONENTS AND SERVICES (15)

(includes sports equipment)
DIKAR
Urarte Kales, 26
Apdo. 193
(pol. Ind. San Lorenzo)
20570 Bergara
(Guipuzcoa)
Tel: (43) 76 54 40
Fax: (43) 76 51 42
ACTIVITIES:
Muzzle-loading weapons. Sports

rifles. Tents. Physical fitness equipment.

EREDU
Ola Auzoa, 4
20250 Legorreta
(Guipuzcoa)
Tel: (43) 80 61 00
80 62 75
Fax: (43) 80 63 74
ACTIVITIES:
Metal furniture for the country, garden and beach. Modern interior furniture.

ORBEA
Pol. Ind. Goitondo
48269 Mallabia
(Vizcaya)
Tel: (43) 17 19 50
Fax: (43) 17 43 97
ACTIVITIES:
Bicycles.

EDERFIL
Pol Industrial, s/n
20250 Legorreta
(Guipuzcoa)
Tel: (43) 80 60 50
Fax: (43) 80 63 49
ACTIVITIES:
Electrical conductors.

GOIPLAST
B. KATEA
20213 Idiazabal
(Guipuzcoa)
Tel: (43) 80 14 42
Fax: (43) 80 18 62
ACTIVITIES:
Study and transformation of composite material parts. Design and manufacture of resin moulds. Urban fixtures.

HERTELL
Poligono Industrial, s/n
20267 Ikastegieta

(Guipuzcoa)
Tel: (43) 65 32 40
Fax: (43) 65 33 32
ACTIVITIES:
Depressors. Valves Reducers, Pumps.

IRIZAR
San Andrés, 6
20216 Ormaiztegi
(Guipuzcoa)
Tel: (43) 88 19 00
Fax: (43) 88 91 01
ACTIVITIES:
Components for buses

UROLA
Urola-Kalea, s/n
Apdo. 3
20230 Legazpia
(Guipuzcoa)
Tel: (43) 72 43 04
Fax: (43) 72 13 17
ACTIVITIES:
Extrusion, injection and blowing of plastics. Construction of machinery for extrusion-blowing of plastics.

ALECOP
Loramendi, s/n
20500 Mondragon
(Guipuzcoa)
Tel: (43) 79 50 11
Fax: (43) 79 92 12
ACTIVITIES:
Instructional equipment for teaching centres (from primary to university level). Installation of prefabricated systems.

ALKARGO
B. Belako, s/n
Apdo. 102
48100 Mungia
(Vizcaya)
Tel: (4) 674 00 04

Fax: (4) 674 44 17
ACTIVITIES:
Distribution transformers. Medium power transformers. Autotransformers.

COINALDE
Concejo, 10
01013 Vitoria
(Alva)
Tel: (45) 26 42 88
26 42 99
Fax: (45) 25 39 97
ACTIVITIES:
Nails. Wire. Metal meshwork.

DANONA LITOGRAFIA
Pol. Ugaldetxo, s/n
20180 Oiartzun
(Guipuzcoa)
Tel: (43) 49 12 50
49 10 87
49 11 29
Fax: (43) 49 16 60
ACTIVITIES:
Catalogues. Magazines. Books. Posters. Calendars. Leaflets.

ELKAR
Autonomia, 71-3.
48012 Bilbao
(Vizcaya)
Tel: (4) 427 33 00
427 33 70
Fax: (4) 427 40 97
ACTIVITIES:
Industrial catalogues. Books. Advertising leaflets. Magazines. General graphical products.

OIARSO
Pol. Ind. Ugaldetxo
Parcela 12
20180 Oiartzun
(Guipuzcoa)

Tel: (43) 49 16 27
49 12 52
Fax: (43) 49 26 37
ACTIVITIES:
Infusion
equipment.
Transfusion
equipment.
Catheters.
Epicraneals.
Enteral nutrition.
Parenteral
nutrition.
Accessories and
connectology.
Probes and
anaesthesia
equipment.

OSATU
Traveia de Padure,
s/n
48240 Berriz
(Vizcaya)
Tel: (4) 622 53 71
622 53 99
Fax: (4) 622 53 91
ACTIVITIES:
Monitors. Mono-
and three-
channels
electrocardiographs.
Defibrillators.
Ergometry.

**F. CONSTRUCTION
DIVISION (8)**

BIURRARENA
Pol. Bidebitarte
Donostia Ibilbidea, 28
Apdo. 887
20014 Astigarraga
Tel: (43) 55 43 50
Fax: (43) 55 53 60
ACTIVITIES:
Machinery and
after sales service
for Public works
and forestry.
Maintenance and
industrial supplies-
hydraulic and
pneumatic
material.

ROCHMAN
48210 Ochandiano
(Vizcaya)
Tel: (45) 45 00 75
Fax: (45) 45 02 57
ACTIVITIES:
Conveyor belt
rolls. Handling
equipment. Heat-
shrink packaging
equipment.

URSSA
Campo de los
Palacios, 18
Apdo. 284
01006 Vitoria
(Alava)
Tel: (45) 13 57 44
Fax: (45) 13 57 92
ACTIVITIES:
Engineering,
manufacture of
metallic structures.
Extruded PVC
profiles.

ORONA
Pol. Ind. Lastaola
20120 Hernani
(Guipuzcoa)
Tel: (43) 55 14 00
Fax: (43) 55 00 47
ACTIVITIES:
Manufacture and
installation of
elevators and
escalators.

COVIMAR
B. Leguineche
Apdo. 20
48340 Amorebieta
(Vizcaya)
Tel: (4) 673 05 46
Fax: (4) 673 44 91
ACTIVITIES:
Work surfaces
and funerary art.
Processed
material. Laying. In
marble granite and
stone.

ETORKI
Pol. Ind Murga, 16

01479 Murga-Aiala
(Alava)
Tel: (45) 39 90 72
Fax: (45) 39 92 23
ACTIVITIES:
Pine boards and
planks.

LANA
C/ Santxolopetegui
Auzoa, 24
20560 Onati
(Guipuzcoa)
Tel: (43) 78 01 11
Fax: (43) 78 32 22
ACTIVITIES:
Formwork boards.
Do-it-yourself
boards.
Prefabricated
housing.

VICON
Padre Larroca, 3
20001 San
Sebastian
(Guipuzcoa)
Tel: (43) 27 03 00
Fax: (43) 27 30 47
ACTIVITIES:
Buildings and
homes. Factory
premises
ACTIVITIES:
PVC doors and
windows. Elgeta
(Guipuzcoa)
Tel: (43) 78 90 22
Fax: (43) 78 90 24

**G. HOUSEHOLD
GOODS-
DOMESTIC
APPLIANCES (6)**

**FAGOR
ELECTRODOMESTICOS**
B. San Andrés, s/n
Apdo. 49
20500 Mondragon
(Guipuzcoa)
Tel: San Andrés:
(43) 79 52 22
Fax: San Andrés:
(43) 79 68 81

Tel. Garagarza:
(43) 79 27 44
Fax. Garagarza:
(43) 79 68 91
ACTIVITIES:
Cookers. Ovens.
Fridges. Washing
machines.
Dishwashers.
Freezers.
Microwave ovens.
Extractor hoods.
Dryers. Water
heaters. Air
conditioning.
Storage heaters.
Cookware. Small
domestic
appliances.

COINMA
Vitoriabidea, 4-Z.I.
Ali-Gobeo
01010 Vitoria
(Alava)
Tel: (45) 24 16 16
Fax: (45) 24 06 37
ACTIVITIES:
Wooden furniture
for the office and
home.

DANONA
B. Lasao, s/n
Apdo. 42
20730 Azpeitia
(Guipuzcoa)
Tel: (43) 81 59 00
Fax: (43) 81 00 66
ACTIVITIES:
Veneered lounge
furniture. Bedroom
and children's
bedroom furniture.

HERRIOLA
Okamika
Industrialdea
48289
Gizaburuaga
(Vizcaya)
Tel: (4) 684 29 50
Fax: (4) 684 29 05
ACTIVITIES:
Modern style
lighting.

FAGOR
INDUSTRIAL
Barrio
Sancholopetegui n.
22
Apdo. 17
20560 Onati
(Guipuzcoa)
Tel: (43) 78 01 51
Fax: (43) 78 07 66
ACTIVITIES:
Dishwashers,
Glass washers.
washing
machines, gas and
electric cookers.
Boilers. Steam
convection ovens,
fryers.

KIDE
Pol. Gardotza, s/n
Berriatua
Apdo. 61
Ondarroa
(Vizcaya)
Tel: (4) 683 16 00
Fax: (4) 683 31 33
ACTIVITIES:
Cold storage units.

H. SUBSIDIARY
COMPANIES (13)
(Formed as joint
stock companies
and not as
cooperatives)

CIMA
(80% owned by
Fagar Sistemas)
Parc d'activites le
Pradines, Orange
France
Tel: (33) 90 111 660
Fax: (33) 90 511
887
ACTIVITIES:
Consulting for
automated building
systems.

COPRECI DE
MEXICO, S.A.
(40% owned by
Copreci)

C/ Uno, #736 Z.I.
Guadalajara
Jalisco-Mexico
44940
Tel: 52 36 610 60 65
Fax: 52 36 610 60
46
ACTIVITIES:
Manufacture of
valves for gas
barbecues

EXTRA
ELECTROMENAGER
(51% owned by
Fagor
Electrodomesticos)
Avenue Hassan II
Mohammedia
BP 179-Morocco
Tel:(212) (3) 32 74
12
Fax: (212) (3) 32
74 25
ACTIVITIES:
Manufacture of
refrigerators.

FAGOR
(THAILAND) LTD.
(70% owned by
Fagor Electronica)
Wellgrow
Industrial Estate
82 Moo 5 Bangna-
Trad
Highway Km 36
Tambol
Bangsamak
Chachoegsao
24130
(THAILAND)
Tel: 66 38 57 00 89
Fax: 66 38 57 00 91
ACTIVITIES:
Manufacture of
electrical
alternators

FERROPLAST
(51% owned by
Maier)
Apdo. 6015
36210 Vigo
Tel: (86) 29 00 07
Fax: (86) 23 88 04

ACTIVITIES:
Injection of
thermoplastics

FRESH
ENGINEERING
(50% owned by
Fagor
Electrodomesticos)
24 Mohamed el
Harouny St. NASR
CITY
P.O. Box 7112-
NASR
CITY
Cairo (Egypt)
Tel: 07 202 274 53
84
Fax:07 202 274 54
25
ACTIVITIES:
Manufacture of
washers and gas
heaters.

ISEI, S.A.
(81.4% owned by
Fagor Sistemas)
Ama Kandida, 21
(Denac)
20140
(Guipuzcoa)
Tel: (43) 59 44 00
Fax: (43) 59 05 36
ACTIVITIES:
Systems and
services for
information
technology.

OMICO
(50% owned by
Copreci)
B. San Andres, s/n
Apdo. 49
20500 Mondragon
(Guipuzcoa)
ACTIVITIES:
Racks for
household
appliances.

MC LEAN, S.A.
(70% owned by
Fagor
Electrodomesticos)

Valentin Gomez.
151
1706 Haedo,
Buenos Aires
(Argentina)
Tel: (54) (1) 483
07 31
Fax: (54) (1) 654
02 58
ACTIVITIES:
Manufacture of
household
applliances

P.I PROIN, S.A.
(100% owned by
Fagor Arrasate)
Avda. Carlos, 10-1
San Sebastian
(Spain)
Tel:(43) 45 25 00
Fax: (43)46 29 33
ACTIVITIES:
Manufacture of
machine tools

SEI, FAGOR
(66.6% owned by
Fagor Sistemas)
Le Forum
64116 Bayonne
CEDEX
(France)
Tel:(33) 59 58 00 00
Fax: (33) 59 58 01
99

SWITCH
CONTROLS
(100% owned by
Copreci)
Mercuriusstrat, 3
P.O. Box 147-6500
AC
Nijmegen (Holland)
Tel: 31 24 377 59 44
Fax: 31 24 377 47 85
ACTIVITIES:
Electric Switches
for washers

TIANJIN IRIZAR
COACH
(35.7% owned by
Irizar)
218 Hong Qi

Nankai District
Tianjin (China)
Tel:(86) 022 761
30 41
Fax:(86) 022 761
33 45
ACTIVITIES:
Manufacture of
buses

**III.
DISTRIBUTION
GROUP (8)**

**COMMERCIAL
EREIN**
Pol Ibur Erreka, s/n
20600 Eibar
(Guipuzcoa)
Tel: (43) 11 85 44
Fax: (43) 11 86 34
ACTIVITIES:
Marketing of food
products to
catering industry
and communities.

CONSUM
Avda. de Espioca,
s/n
46400 Silla
(Valencia)
Tel: (6) 197 40 50
Fax: (6) 197 40 92
ACTIVITIES:
Consumer grocery
wholesale-retailing
in large and small
sales outlets.

EROSKI
B. San Agustin, s/n
48230 Elorrio
(Vizcaya)
Tel: (4) 621 12 11
Fax. (4) 621 12 26
ACTIVITIES:
Consumer grocery
wholesale-retailing
(Cleaning
products. Textiles.
Domestic
appliances. Travel.
Fish. Groceries.
Liquids. Frozen
food)

**EROSMER
(Holding
Company)**
Travesia de Rodil,
107
20013 San
Sebastian
Tel: (43) 28 63 09
Fax: (43) 28 60 23
ACTIVITIES:
Construction and
acquisition of
food-retail outlets

AUZO-LAGUN
Ctra. Garagarza, s/n
20500 Mondragon
(Guipuzcoa)
Tel: (43) 79 46 56
Fax: (43) 79 43 66
ACTIVITIES:
Catering and
cleaning services.

BARRENETXE
Okerra 7
48270 Markina
(Vizcaya)
Tel: (4) 616 81 43
ACTIVITIES:
Greenhouse and
open-air
agriculture
(lettuce, tomatoes
peppers etc.

BEHI-ALDE
Olaeta-Aramaiona
(Alava)
Apdo. 44
Mondragon
Tel: (45) 45 01 00
Farm: (45) 45 01 00
ACTIVITIES:
Milk and dairy
cattle.

MIBA
Ctra. Etxebarria, s/n
48270 Markina
(Vizcaya)
Tel: (4) 616 78 84
Fax: (4) 616 78 86
Olaeta-Aramaiona
(Alava)

FARM: (45) 45 02
59
ACTIVITIES:
Manufacture of
compound feeds.
Sale of seeds,
fertilizers and
plant products.
Hardware and
small agricultural
machinery. Milking
and farming
installations.
Veterinary
service. Pig
fattening and
breeding.

**IV.
CORPORATE
ACTIVITIES (15)**

(Includes research
and education)

IDEKO
Poligono Industrial
Barrio Arriaga-
Apdo. 80
20870 Elgoibar
(Guipuzcao)
Tel: (43) 74 25 54
Fax: (43) 74 36 74
ACTIVITIES:
Technical
services.
Mechanical
engineering.
Information
technology.
Production
engineering.
Control
engineering.

IKERLAN
Technological
Research Centre
José Maria
Arrizmendiarrieta
Pasalekua, n. 2-
Apdo. 146
20500 Mondragon
(Guipuzcoa)
Tel: (43) 77 12 00
Fax: (43) 79 69 44

ACTIVITIES:
Information
technology. Design
and manufacturing
technology.
Energy research.

MTC
Poligono Industrial
Arabieta
48300 Gernika
(Vizcaya)
Tel: (4) 625 56 25
Fax: (4) 625 53 84
ACTIVITIES:
Research and
development of
thermoplastics.

ETEO
Business College
Larrana, 33
20560 Onate
(Guipuzcoa)
Tel: (43) 78 13 11
ACTIVITIES:
Business
education

LEA-ARTIBAI
Avda. Jemein, 19
48270 Marquina
(Vizcaya)
Tel: (4) 616 75 52
Fax: (4) 616 66 74
ACTIVITIES:
Technical
education

**MONDRAGON
ESKOLA
POLITEKNIKOA
(Polytechnical
University)**
C/Loramendi, 4
20500 Mondragon
(Guipuzcoa)
Tel: (43) 79 47 00
Fax: (43) 79 15 36
ACTIVITIES:
University Level
degrees,
specializing in
engineering
related programs.
OTALORA

Palacio OTALORA
Barrio
Aretzabaleta
20550
Aretzabaleta
(Guipuzcoa)
Tel: (43) 79 79 99
Fax: (43) 77 07 88
ACTIVITIES:
Cooperative and
general business
formation/
education
-managers and
boards.

**TXORIERRI
POLITEKNIKA
IKASTEGIA**
Barrio Arteaga n.
22
48012 Derio
(Vizcaya)
Tel: (4) 453 10 41
ACTIVITIES:
Technical
education

SAIOLAN
C/Loramendi, 4
20500 Mondragon
(Guipuzcoa)
Tel: (43) 79 02 11
Fax: (43) 79 15 36
ACTIVITIES:
Identification and
promotion of new
business
activities.

ASCORP
Rosario Pino, 1
28020 Madrid
(Madrid)
Tel: (1) 579 06 04
Fax: (1) 570 73 04
ACTIVITIES:
Investment
Company

**MCC
INTERNATIONAL**
José Maria
Arrizmendiarrieta
Pasalekua, n. 5
20500 Mondragon

(Guipuzcoa)
Tel: (43) 77 93 00
Fax: (43) 79 66 32
ACTIVITIES:
Foreign
Commercial
Activity

FUNDACION MCC
José Maria
Arrizmendiarrieta
Pasalekua, n. 5
20500 Mondragon
(Guipuzcoa)
Tel: (43) 77 93 00
Fax: (43) 79 66 32
ACTIVITIES:
Promotion of the
social economy

**MCC
INVERSIONES**
José Maria
Arrizmendiarrieta
Pasalekua, n. 5
20500 Mondragon
(Guipuzcoa)
Tel: (43) 77 93 00
Fax: (43) 79 66 32
ACTIVITIES:
Investments -
financing and
promoting
business
enterprises

MCC
José Maria
Arrizmendiarrieta
Pasalekua, n. 5
20500 Mondragon
(Guipuzcoa)
Tel: (43) 77 93 00
Fax: (43) 79 66 32
ACTIVITIES:
Overall
Coordination of all
Mondragon
member
enterprises

MCC SUSTRAI
José Maria
Arrizmendiarrieta
Pasalekua, n. 5
20500 Mondragon

(Guipuzcoa)
Tel: (43) 77 93 00
Fax: (43) 79 66 32
ACTIVITIES:
Commercial Real
Estate

APPENDIX III

USEFUL ADDRESSES MENTIONED IN TEXT

Publications:
Lankide (the official Mondragon magazine)
Otalora
Azatza, 20550 Aretxabaleta
Gipuzkoa, Spain
fax. 43) 77-07-88

Vida Cooperativa (offical magazine of Valencia group)
Centre d'Educacio Cooperativa
Universidad Florida
Apartat 15
46470 Catarroja (Valencia)
fax 126-99-33

Making Waves Magazine
Centre for Community Enterprise
2905-31ST St.
Suite 5
Vernon, B.C. V1T 5H6
Canada
FAX 250) 542-7229

Atlantic Cooperator
P.O. Box 1386
Antigonish, N.S.
Canada   B2G 2L7
FAX 902) 863-8077
atlcoop@atcon.com

Center for the Study of Cooperatives
University of Saskatchewan
101 Diefenbaker Place
Saskatoon
Saskatchewan
Canada S79 5BS
Fax. 306) 966-8517

New View Productions
(Video and booklet series on Community Business)
P.O. Box 1201
Sydney, N.S.
Canada B1P 6J9
FAX. 902)567-0153
bca@uccb.ns.ca

Other Contacts

Inaki Idiazabal Loinaz
Relaciones Cooperativas
Otalora
20550 Aretxaaleta
Gipuzkoa
Spain
fax 43) 77-07-88
otalora2@sarenet.es

Jose Portillo
Director of Informatica
Florida Centro de formacion
Apartat de Correos 15
46470 Catarroja
Valencia
tel 6— 126-6400/61
fax 6)- 126-9933
email jportilla@florida-uni.es

Caixa Popular
Parc Tecnologic
Calle 1, Sector Este
tel 011-34-6-131-82-82
fax 131-81-82
46980 PATERNA
Valencia

Rommel Gonzalez Diaz
Calle 38 No 327 X 35A
Fraccionmiento del N orte Chenku
Merida, Yucatan
Mexico
tel 99) 87-27-89
Codigo Postal 97219

Greg MacLeod
University College of Cape Breton
Box 5300   TEL 902-562-2420
Sydney, N.S.   fAX 902-567-0153
Canada B1P 6L2   gmacleod@uccb.ns.ca

Gert MacIntyre
Director
Community Economic Development Institute
University College of Cape Breton
                         BCA HOLDINGS
                         BOX 1201
                         SYDNEY, N.S.
                         CANADA   B1P 6J9
                         tel 902) 539-1777
                         fax   539-5107
                         BCA@uccb.ns.ca

New Dawn Enterprises
P.O. Box 1055
Sydney, N.S.
Canada   B1P 6J7
Tel. 902) 539-9560
fax 902) 539-7210

GNP Development Corporation
P.O. BOX 69
Plum Point
Newfoundland
Canada   A0K 4A0
FAX 709) 247-2324
TEL 709) 247-2354

Raul Hernandez Garciadiego
Director General
Alternativas y Procesos de Participacion Social A.C.
Tel. and fax (238) 2-50-65 y 2-41-97
Calle Vicente Guerrero 141,
San Lorenzo Teotipilco,
Apartado Postal 306 Tehuacan 75700
Mexico
E-Mail: alternativ@laneta.apc.org

Websites
www.idrc.ca
www.mondragon.mcc.es
www.florida-uni.es (for Valencia experiment)
www.bca.uccb.ns.ca

BIBLIOGRAPHY

Aguiree, Inaki. *Ocio Acivo v Tercera Edad*. Mondragon: Caja Laboral, 1981.

Aldabaldetreacu, F., and J. Gray. *De L'Artisanat Industriel au Complexe Coopératif: L'Experience de Mondragon*. Paris: Centre de Recherches Cooperatives, 1967.

Ash, M. "Reflections on Mondragon." *Town and Country Planning* 47 (1979): 11-14.

Aranjuren, Jose Luis L. "Conceptions of the Economic and Moral Life." *Trahabo y Union* Dec. 1989.

Arrizmendiarrieta. Mondragon: Ceja Laboral Popular, 1984.

Arrizmendiarrietta, Don José Maria. *Escritos de Don José Maria Arizmendi-Arrista*. Ed. Mendizabal. Mondragon: Caja Laboral, 1978.

Axworthy, Christopher S. "Mondragon: A Less Favorable Assessment." *Radical   Perspectives on Social Problems*. New York: General Hall, 1986.

Azurmendi, José. *El Hombre Cooperativo*. Mondragon: Caja Laboral Popular, 1985.

Barton, D. "Mondragon: Experiment or Prototype?"*Accountancy* 93 (1982): 125-26.

Berger, Lisa and Chris Clamp. "Striking Similarities: Spain." *Workplace Democracy* 10.4 (1983): 4+.

Boyle, George. *Father Tompkins of Nova Scotia*. New York: P.J. Kenedy, 1953.

Bradley, Keith, and Alan Gelb. *Cooperation at Work: The Mondragon Experience*. London: Heinemann Educational Books, 1983.

—. "Cooperative Labour Relations: Mondragon's Response to Recession." *British Journal of Industrial Relations* 25 (1987): 77-97.

—. *"Mixed Economy" versus "Cooperative" Adjustment: Mondragon's experience through Spain's Recession*. DRD 122. Washington: World Bank, 1985.

—. "Motivation and Control in the Mondragon Experiment." *British Journal of Industrial Relations* 19.2 (1981): 211-231.

—. "The Mondragon Cooperatives: Guidelines for a Cooperative Economy *Participatory and Self-Managed Firms*. Ed. D.C. Jones and J. Svejnar. Massachusetts: Lexington Books, 1982.

—. "The Replicability and Sustainability of the Mondragon Experiment." *British Journal of Industrial Relations* 20.1 (1982): 20-33.

Caja Laboral Popular. *Annual Report 1980-1996.* Mondragon: Spain CLP.

Campbell, A. *Mondragon 1980.* London: Industrial Common Ownership Movement, 1980.

Campbell, A., and B. Foster. *The Mondragon Movement.* ICOM Pamphlet 5. London:Industrial Common Ownership Movement, 1980.

Campbell, Alistair, et al. W*orker-Owners: The Mondragon Achievement.* London: Anglo-German Foundation for the Study of Industrial Society, 1977.

Clamp, Chris. "Managing Cooperation at Mondragon." *Proceedings of the National Employee-Ownership and Participation Conference.* Greensbro: Guilford College, 1984: 244-251.

—. "Managing Cooperation at Mondragon." Ph.D. diss., Boston College, 1986.

—. "Mondragon Meets the Recession." *Workplace Democracy* 10.2 (1984): 10-11.

Clutterbuck, D. "Where Industrial Cooperatives Reign in Spain." *International Management* 29 (1974): 35-40.

Cort, John. "The Marvels of Mondragon." *Commonweal* 18 June 1982: 369-71.

del Arco, José Luis. *El Complejo Cooperativo de Mondragon.* Madrid: Associatión de Estudios Cooperativos, 1982.

Eaton, J. "The Basque Workers' Cooperatives." *Industrial Relations Journal* 10: 32-40, 1979.

—. *The Mondragon Cooperatives.* London: Centre for Alternative Industrial and Technological Systems, 1978.

—. "The Relevance of Mondragon to Britain." *Political Quarterly* 49 (1978): 478-83.

Elena Diaz, Fernando. *Quince Anõs de la Ex periencial de la Zona de Mondragon* no 476. Madrid: Información Comercial Española, Ministerio de Economia y Hacienda, 1973.

Ellerman, David. "Entrepreneurship in the Mondragon Cooperatives." *Review of Social Economy* 42 (1984): 272-94.

—. *Management Planning with Labor as a Fixed Cost: The Mondragon Annual Business Plan Manual.* Somerville, MA: Industrial Cooperative Association, 1984.

—. "The Mondragon Cooperative Movement." *Harvard Business School* case no. 1-384-270. Boston: Harvard Business School, 1984.

—. *The Socialization of Entrepreneurship: The Empresarial Division of the Caja Laboral Popular.* Somerville, MA: Industrial Cooperative Association, 1982.

Franklin, Ursula. *The Real World of Technology.* Toronto: CBC Enterprises, 1990.

Friedman, Milton. *Capitalism and Freedom.* Chicago: University of Chicago Press, 1962.

—. *Free to Choose.* New York: Harcourt Brace, 1980.

García, Quintin. *Les Coopératives Industrielles de Mondragon.* Paris: Editions Ouvieres, 1970.

Gardner, David. "Cooperative Experiment A Success." *Financial Times* 10 June 1982.

Gorroño, Inaki. "Our Experiment and International Cooperation," visit of Rt. Hon. Kenneth Clark, P.C., M.P., Minister of Employment of the United Kingdom. Mondragon, CLP.

—. *Experiencia Cooperativa en el Pais Vasco.* Durango, Spain: Leopoldo Zugaza, 1975.

—. "L'Experience Cooperative de Mondragon." *Cooperatives et Developpement* 17 (1985): 2.

Gower, L.C.B. *The Principles of Modern Company Law.* London: Stevens and Sons, 1969.

Goyder, M. "The Mondragon Experiment." *Personal Management* 11 (1979): 24-27.

Gui, Benedetto. "Basque versus Illyrian Labor-Managed Firms: The Problem of Property Rights." *Journal of Comparative Economics* 8 (1984): 168-181.

Gutiérrez-Johnson Ana. "Compensation, Equity, and Industrial Democracy in the Mondragon Cooperatives." *Economic Analysis and Workers' Self Management* 12 (1978): 267-89.

—. "Cooperativism and Justice: A Study and Cross-Cultural Comparison of Preferences for Forms of Equity among Basque Students of a Cooperative School-Factory." M.S. thesis, Cornell University, 1976.

—. "Industrial Democracy in Action: The Cooperative Complex of Mondragon." Ph.D. diss., Cornell University, 1982.

—. "The Mondragon Model of Cooperative Enterprise." *Changing Work* 1 (1984): 35-41.

Gutiérrez-Johnson, Ana, and William Foote Whyte. "The Mondragon System of Worker Production Cooperatives." *Industrial and Labor Relations Review* 31.1 (1977): 18-30.

Gutiérrez-Marquez, Antonio. "The Creation of Industrial Cooperatives in the Basque Country." Ph.D. diss., University of Chicago, 1985.

Hacker, Sally. *Pleasure, Power and Technology*. New York: Routledge, 1992.

Industrial Cooperative Association. "Report on a Study Visit to Mondragon." Unpublished manuscript, 1984.

Información Comercial Española. *El Coopertivismo Industrial de Mondragon* no. 467-68. Madrid: Información Comercial Española, Ministerio de Economia y Hacienda, 1972.

Jackobs, Steven Curtis. "Community, Industrial Democracy, and the Cooperatives of Mondragon" B.A. thesis, Harvard University, 1979.

Jay, P. "St. George and Mondragon." *Times* 7 April 1977.

——. "Til We Have Built Mondragon." *Times* 7 April 1977.

Job Ownership Ltd. *Lagun-Aro: The Non-Profit Making Social Welfare Mutuality of the Mondragon Cooperatives*. London: Job Ownership, 1982.

John Paul II. *Laborem Exercens*. Rome, 1981.

Kaswan, Jacques, and Ruth Kaswan. *The Mondragon Cooperatives-1986: Economic Democracy*. Berkeley, Calif.: Alternatives Center.

Laidlaw, Alex. *The Campus and Community*. Montreal: Harvest, 1961.

——. *The Man from Margaree*. Toronto: McClelland and Stewart, 1971.

Larranaga, Jesús. *Buscando un Camino: Don José María Arrizmendi-Arrieta y la Experiencia cooperativa de Mondragon*. Bilbao, Spain: R&F, 1981.

——. *Don José María Arrizmendiarrieta y la Experiencia Cooperativa de Mondragon*. Mondragon: Ceja Laboral Popular, 1981.

——. "José Ayala: Con la Muerte a Cuestas." *Unión Lankide* Oct. 1992: 8-9. Larañaga, Juan. *El Consejo Social: Pasado, Presente y Futuro*. Mondragon: Caja Laboral Popular, 1986.

"Local Employment Initiatives in a Rural Framework." *Local Development Paper Series*. Ottawa: Economic Council of Canada, 1989.

Logan, C. "The Mondragon Cooperative Model: A Critical Appraisal." *Public Enterprise* 16 (1979): 7-8.

MacIntyre, Gertrude Anne. *Active Partners: Education and Local Development*. Sydney: UCCB Press, 1995.

MacLeod, Greg. *New Age Business*. Ottawa: Canadian Council on Social Development, 1986.

Milbrath, Robert. "Institutional Development and Capital Accumulation in a Complex of Basque Worker Cooperatives (Spain)." Ph.D. diss., University of Michigan, 1986.

—. "Lessons from the Mondragon Cooperatives." *Science for the People* 15 (1983) 3+.

—. "Long-Run Accumulation of Capital in a Cooperative Sector: Simulation Analysis Based on the Case of Mondragon." *Proceedings of the National Employee-*
Ownership and Participation Conference. Greensboro, N.C.: Guilford College, 1984.

Mollner, Terence Jerome. "Mondragon: A Third Way." *Review of Social Economy* 42 (1984): 260-71.

—. "The Design of a Nonformal Education Process to Establish a Community Development Program Basd upon Mahatma Gandhi's Theory of Trusteeship." Ph.D. diss., University of Massachusetts, 1982.

Mondragon. Mondragon: Caja Laboral Popular, 1981.

Mondragon Cooperatives - Myth or Model. England: Cooperatives Research Unit, Open University, 1982.

Morrison, Roy. *We Build the Road as We Travel.* Philadelphia: New Society Publishers, 1991.

Morrison, Roy, and Judy Elliot, trans. *Principios Basicos de la Experiencia Coopertiva de Mondragon.* Mondragon: Lankide, 1987.

Nairn, Allan. "Mondragon: Where Workers Call the Shots: An Alternative to Multinationals." *Multinational Monitor* 5 (1984): 9-31.

Oakeshott, Robert. "European Cooperatives: Perspectives from Spain." *Prospects for Workers' Cooperatives in Europe: Volume II.* Brussels: Commission of the European Communities, 1981: S1-S22.

—. "Industrial Cooperatives: The Middle Way." *Lloyds Bank Review* 227 (1978): 44-58.

—. "Mondragon: Spain's Oasis of Democracy." *Observer (London) Supplement* 21 Jan 1973.

—. "The Mondragon Group." *The Case for Workers Co-ops.* London: Routledge and Kegan Paul, 1978.

—. "The Mondragon Model of Participation." *Industrial and Commercial Training* 10 (1978): 50-56.

Ormaechea, José María. *El Hombre que yo Conocí.* Mondragon: Fundación Gizabidea, 1986.

Ornelas-Navarro, Jesús Carlos. "Cooperative Production and Technical Education in the Basque County." *Prospects* 13. (1982): 467-475.

—. "Producer Cooperatives and Schooling: The Case of Mondragon." Ph.D. diss., Stanford University, 1980.

Pérez de Calleja, Basterrechea A. *The Group of Cooperatives at Mondragon in the Spanish Basque Country*. Mondragon: Caja Laboral Popular, 1975.

Perry, Stewart. *Communities on the Way*. Albany: State University of New York Press, 1987.

Piore, M. J. and C. F. Sabel. *Second Industrial Divide: Possibilities for Prosperity*. New York: Basic Books, 1984.

Porter, Michael. *Competitive Advantage*. New York: Free Press, 1984.

Porter, Michael J., and Charles F. Sabel. "Italian Small Business Development: Lessons for U.S. Industrial Policy." *American Industry in International Competition: Government Policies and Corporate Strategies*. Ithaca, N.Y.: Cornell University Press, 1983.

Quarter, Jack. *The Canadian Social Economy*. Toronto: Lorimer, 1992. Royal Arsenal Cooperative Society Ltd. *Mondragon: The Basque Cooperatives*. London: Royal Arsenal Cooperative Society Ltd., 1980.

Saive, Marie-Anne. "Cooperative Doctrine and Rent in Mondragon." *Annals of Public and Cooperative Economy* 52 (1981): 369-79.

—. "Mondragon: An Experiment with Cooperative Development in the Industrial Sector." *Annals of Public and Cooperative Economy* 51(1980): 223-55.

Sdervy, Pierre. *Les Cooperatives de Mondragon*. France: Societe Inter-Professions Service, 1957.

Sperry, Charles W. "What Makes Mondragon Work?" *Review of Social Economy* 43 (1985): 345-56.

Stahl, Gerry. "Education for Democracy at Mondragon." *Workplace Democracy* 11.3 (1984): 110-113. *The Mondragon Experiment*. Mondragon: Caja Laboral Popular, 1985.

Textos Basicos de Otalora- (a series of 12 booklets outlining the basic philosophy of the Mondragon experiment written by various Mondragon authors)- Azatza, Aretxabaleta, 1994 .

Thomas, Henk. "The Distribution of Earnings and Capital in the Mondragon Cooperatives." *Economic Analysis and Workers' Management* 14 (1980): 363-92.

—. "The Dynamics of Social Ownership: Some Considerations in the Perspective of the Mondragon Experience." *Economic Analysis and Workers' Management* 19 (1985): 147-60.

—. "The Performance of the Mondragon Cooperatives in Spain." *Participatory and Self-managed Firms*. Ed. D. Jones and J Svejnar. Massachusettes: Lexington Books,1982.

Thomas, Henk, and Chris Logan. *Mondragon: An Economic Analysis*. London: Allen & Unwin, 1982.

—. *Mondragon Producer Cooperatives.* The Hague: Intsitute of Social Sciences, 1980.

Vines S. "A Mondragon for Wales?" *Observer (London)* 8 Feb 1981.

Wellens, John. "Worker Owners: The Mondragon Achievement." *Industrial and Commercial Training* 10 (1978): 57-59.

Wilkinson, Paul, and Jack Quarter. *The Evangeline Cooperative Experience.* Toronto: University of Toronto Press, 1996.

White D. "Successful Basque Cooperatives: The Unorthodox Survivor." *Financial Times* 22 May 1984.

Whyte, William Foote. "Social Inventions for Solving Human Problems." *American Sociological Review* 47 (1982): 1-13.

Whyte, William Foote, and Kathleen King Whyte. *Making Mondragon: The Growth and Dynamics of the Mondragon Cooperative Complex.* Ithaca, N.Y.: Cornell University ILR Press, 1988.

"Working Paper: Organization for Economic Cooperation and Development." *ILE Program - Organization for Economic Cooperation and Development (OECD).* Paris: 1989.

Zwerdling, D. "Mondragon of Spain." *Workplace Democracy.* New York: Harper & Row, 1980.

INDEX